DRAGON

But what if I'm a mermaid
In these jeans of his
With her name still on it
Hey but I don't care
Cause sometimes
I said sometimes
I hear my voice
And it's been here
Silent all these years

Tori Amos
'Silent All These Years'*

Dragon King's Daughter

Adventures of a Sex and Love Addict

RUTH PHYPERS

First published in 2016
by

Mud Pie Books
43 Leckford Road, Oxford OX2 6HY
Registered Co No.4405635

ISBN 978-0-9934770-5-8

For my mother and father.
And all my 'girls'. You know who you are…

Author's note

In sharing this personal account of my life I have sought to tell only my story, not other people's. Some names are real, some are not. Sometimes I have changed identifying details. Sometimes I have only shared part of the story. Throughout, I have tried to be discreet whilst remaining authentic. Everything is to the best of my memory.

Contents

The Story of the Dragon King's Daughter

from the *Lotus Sutra*

Once upon a time there was a great Dragon King by the name of Sagara who dwelt in a mystical palace far beneath the sea. King Sagara was deeply admired and respected by his subjects. He possessed many powers, even the ability to cause rain. Yet he and his people lived in fear of the terrifying Garuda bird, their mortal enemy, for the Garuda bird fed on the flesh of dragons.

The King was wise and loving, and he especially treasured his daughter, Naga, the Dragon Girl, whom he protected with his life. He warned her to stay beneath the waves, safe from the attack of the Garuda bird. Naga dutifully obeyed her father, though she often gazed longingly towards the rays of light that pierced the water's surface, illuminating the world above. It wasn't fair, she thought, that her brothers were able to come and go as they pleased. She dreamed of a life where she could breathe in the air and feel the sun on her face.

Sometimes Naga's father would brave outside in search of enlightenment. He would join with her seven Dragon King uncles and together they would make a perilous journey to the mountain retreat of Eagle Peak. Here they would gather and listen to the Buddha, who taught the enlightenment of all living beings. Naga begged to go with him on these journeys but Sagara said that he could not risk her being harmed, such was his love. Instead, he promised to teach Naga everything he heard, word for word. So she would wait excitedly for his return, knowing that great lessons would follow.

One day King Sagara returned from Eagle Peak, his eyes sparkling. He called for Naga. 'We will soon welcome a special guest,' he told her. 'Bodhisattva Manjushri, one of the Buddha's most learned disciples, is coming here to teach us. Manjushri is regarded as the perfection of wisdom, and we must prepare for his arrival.' Naga could hardly contain her excitement. Although so young, she understood the importance of this event. Maybe now she would gain the wisdom she needed to face the world's dangers and be free to explore life on land.

Manjushri arrived riding on the back of a magnificent lion which he left by the water's edge. Naga listened intently as he preached to the entire Sagara kingdom. Manjushri called his teaching the *Lotus Sutra*. This teaching, he said, contained the Buddha's promise of enlightenment for all living beings no matter what their form. It had remained hidden until now, he explained, because it was so revolutionary. The Dragon King's daughter followed every word. To her the teaching made perfect sense; it was exactly what she knew instinctively, deep in her heart. Of course everyone should be happy, regardless of where they came from or who they were! *Of course everyone should be free!*

Manjushri left the Dragon Palace and returned to Eagle Peak, where he took his place, seated upon a thousand-petalled lotus blossom suspended in the air. One day the Buddha asked Manjushri to tell Shariputra, the most enlightened of the Buddha's followers, about his journey to Sagara and the people he had taught there. Manjushri said that on his journey he had seen many people reveal their enlightened self – including the Dragon King's daughter, Naga. He described her deep compassion for all living beings and her wisdom in all things even though she was only eight years old. Shariputra, in his arrogance, refused to accept it. A girl could never be enlightened, he declared, let alone one so young. Women were impeded by their female form; they had to be reborn as a man in some future lifetime before they could attain Buddhahood.

Listening to his foremost disciple assert such beliefs, the Buddha realized that his teaching was in peril. If the enlightenment of all people in their present form were ever to be believed, something must be done. He must call upon the Dragon Girl to prove her enlightenment in front of these deluded men.

With the Buddha's protection Naga was summoned from the depths of the sea and escorted to the dazzling brightness of Eagle Peak. There she stood, in front of the row of men who looked down on her, convinced that a woman could not reveal Buddhahood. Naga presented a jewel to the Buddha, which he gracefully accepted. Then, with compassion, she turned to Shariputra. 'Watch me!' she said. 'It will be quick!' And in the blink of an eye, she transformed her appearance, performed her bodhisattva duties perfectly, and revealed all the characteristics of a Buddha.

In amazement Shariputra and his fellow disciples witnessed this eight-year-old Dragon Girl proclaim the *Lotus Sutra* to all the living beings. Then they watched her take her seat on the thousand-petalled lotus flower. King Sagara and all the people of the world rejoiced.

And so it came to pass that Naga, the Dragon King's daughter, became the first earthly creature in the *Lotus Sutra* to become a Buddha.

Yet, somehow, as the years passed, the story of the Dragon Girl and the *Lotus Sutra* was lost. In a world full of conflict and unhappiness, women continued to be subjugated, forced to take subservient roles. The essential truth of the teaching was denied, and the Buddha's message became nothing more than a distant dream.

Chapter One

Hell

Hell is in the heart of a person who inwardly despises
his father and disregards his mother.

New Year's Gosho[1]

Imagine a love story where the girl doesn't get the boy, or the girl, and still lives happily ever after. *No way!* I hear you cry. *What's the point of that? We want the girl to get the boy, or girl! It can't be a love story otherwise!* And yes, there was a time when I would most certainly have agreed.

But this is my love story. A twenty-first century love story. And, if I'm honest, it took me a long time to realize it. And even longer to love it…

May 1968. Sunderland, Tyne and Wear. Close to the thrashing North Sea waves that pound the Seaburn shore. Where cool misty sea-frets hug the coastline in summer, and a biting sea breeze tears through raw winter air. My birth was traumatic, I am told; a forceps delivery which left my mother torn, exhausted and spent. Sometimes I imagine the overwhelming sense of trepidation she must have felt in those first days of parenthood. My father too. They were both so young. As a baby I faced anxiety with them, caught between their tense and fearful exchanges, deliberately choking one morning to distract them from their argument at the breakfast table. My father was highly intelligent but he struggled emotionally, his frustration often blowing up from nowhere. My mother cared for him and me in equal amounts, each of us as demanding as the other.

At nine months old I fell seriously ill and was admitted to hospital with a raging temperature and a life-threatening illness. My parents were forced to leave me there for several days, while I lay naked under a fan. Physically I recovered, but the experience left a deep emotional wound. When I returned home I pushed my parents away and they mourned the loss of the affectionate baby they had cuddled only days before. My father could not handle this shift and his frustration developed into a rage that terrified me. *It was all my fault.*

The seaside dominated the early years of my life. I took my first steps on the beach, one day unexpectedly finding my feet and pelting towards the crashing waves. In summer I played for hours on the shore with my baby brother Mark, searching for crabs in the rock pools and making castles with coarse golden sand, which would make us scream when it rubbed against our skin as our mother dried us off. Back at home we sat in front of the coal fire, curled up like mice, drying our hair after bath time. My favourite storybook was *Sleeping Beauty*, with its vivid illustrations depicting a hundred-year sleep in a magical forest hidden from the world. I feared the wicked godmother with her evil spells, but adored the ladies-in-waiting who blessed the Princess, and I desperately admired the courageous Prince who was compelled to love.

When my father came home the atmosphere would change. He brought an air of nervousness and tension, which I couldn't escape. The first time I remember his violence I was three years old. I couldn't sleep one night, and I called out for love. The sound of footsteps at my bedroom door brought hope and relief. Yet he carried me downstairs and smacked me so hard that my head span. Then he took me back to bed and left me there, shivering with fear. This became a pattern. I was taken out of church services for not sitting still, or removed from my own birthday parties for being 'over excited'. When Dad's fractious mood rose up from nowhere it made me want to be sick – such was the churning in my stomach and the ringing in my ears. All I wanted to do was to make it right, but I could never work out how.

Instead I became defiant, scorched with an injustice that flared up easily. I would scream and shout: *You can't tell me what to do! I'm not scared of you!* Once a good Christian family came to our house for tea. Our nativity scene was on the sideboard. I walked past it with my arms held out, threatening to knock it off. My father warned me, 'Ruth, don't you dare!' A green light went off in my head. *Swish!* Kings, shepherds and manger went flying. My father swiped me so fast up the stairs that my feet didn't touch the ground. He left me in my room with the lights off until every one went home.

Nights like this left me feeling so ashamed that I started to think about running away, far away to a place where no one knew who I was and I could start again. Aged four, I found some paving slabs stacked up behind the garden shed and decided to build my own house. *That was the answer!* As I tried to move the slabs to create a wall one fell on my foot and broke it. My screams pierced the neighbourhood like a siren and my mother came running in a desperate panic. Another trip to hospital but this time I was happy. With my leg in plaster the punishments eased for a while. And the attention I received... Even gifts! A window of bliss opened and blew fresh warm air into that dark and lonely room.

The world changed dramatically when my father took a new teaching post and we moved south. I was devastated. I couldn't comprehend life without a beach to run along, bubbling waves to jump over, sandcastles and rock pools and slimy seaweed that smelled so salty and popped with watery satisfaction when you squeezed it. No matter what was happening at home, my heart would always lift with the colours of the sea and the vastness of sky and space. It was freedom. It was life. I begged for us not to leave.

We arrived at our new East Midlands home in the cool summer of 1972. People weren't so friendly here. My mother would cry sometimes. She found it hard to connect with these different neighbours. I would comfort her as best I could. *Don't worry, Mummy, you'll make friends soon.* I made a friend of my own with the girl across the road. But soon her parents divorced and she had to move away. I missed her so much. Then, when I was six, my youngest brother Matthew was born. He was angelic, with a cherubic face and the sweetest smile.

Our family tried to be perfect. We went to church every week and my father taught religion at a school across town. But behind closed doors his rages were frightening and embarrassing. He would melt down sometimes, ranting cruel and angry words at my mother, which blasted through the peaceful neighbourhood on hot sunny afternoons like a megaphone on sports day. My heart would sink and my face flush with humiliation, sensing the raised eyebrows and sniggers from the houses around us. When the scene had run its course Mum would always forgive Dad and things would carry on much the same as before. *Maybe it is my fault*, I thought. Maybe that's why I felt so bad.

Sometimes Mark and I would get 'good hidings', a weapon in my father's armoury. Often I could sense a 'good hiding' brewing. Occasionally it would happen with alarming unpredictability. But always the same sequence of events would play out.

First came the declaration: I was going to 'get a good hiding'. My belly immediately formed in knots and sank endlessly down. Then, a long wait until after our family tea. While everyone pretended to act 'normal' I forced my food down into a tumultuous stomach, then retreated to my room until my father woke up from his post-supper nap. When I heard him coming upstairs my body shook and my heart pounded in my chest as if it would explode. He'd call me in, and as I walked into his bedroom, my head span with adrenaline. My throat choked, strangled of words. Somewhere through the high-pitched ringing in my ears was the order to take off my underpants and lift up my dress. Sometimes I was already sobbing, shaking my head, trembling in fear. If I didn't pull down my pants my father pulled them down for me. Rough. Undignified. And eventually there I was. Over his knee, feeling the painful, repetitive beating of a grown man's hard hand against my skin until blood pounded to the surface and felt like it would erupt. His words of harsh criticism simultaneously rang in my ears. Sometimes I writhed and screamed for him to stop. Sometimes I remained silent, trying to relax into a flaccid state which might not hurt so much, hoping that maybe he'd just give up after a while. Trying to 'zen' out at six years old. *You can't hurt me. I don't feel anything.*

After the beating came the order to get dressed. And then the best and the worst part of all: the hug my father demanded. The best because the ordeal was nearly over; the worst, because my shame was draped like a heavy cape over my shoulders that dragged me down. I buried my head into my father's body and sobbed relentlessly. *I'm sorry, Daddy. I love you. I promise to be better.*

And then finally it was over. I lay on my bed confused, my body stinging from the blows, my head pounding. Then I could pick up books and read myself into a world of sanity and adventure and excitement and hope for a happy world. Soothe my skin with my hands. Touch myself; give myself pleasure to ease away the pain. And then lose myself in dreams that were far from reality. I wished for a magical forest to surround me. To sleep for a hundred years… Hell would be over. For now.

I yearned for a life like the *Famous Five* or the *Secret Seven*, with their constant adventures and tight friendships. At school the studying was easy but I struggled to fit in socially. The children of my parents' religious friends accepted me more readily. While the adults were in church we were marched around the corner to a gloomy hall for Sunday School where we learned about Noah's ark and the miracles of Jesus. A creepy man called Fred was in charge. He would often grab hold of me and tickle me to death, his hands reaching across my body as I squirmed to be set free. I learned every word of *Joseph and his Amazing Technicolour Dreamcoat* and performed it to church audiences, basking in the pale limelight of short-lived praise. Sanctuary at last.

Church and school worlds combined toxically when I was eight. A man from church called Mr. K became my schoolteacher. It was to be the worst year of my life.

Mr. K was also a creepy man. He had a long ginger bushy beard and wore glasses. He smelled odd and wore his trousers pulled up high on his waist. In the same way that there was no one else on television quite like Jimmy Savile, there was no other schoolteacher quite like Mr. K. Punitive one minute, playful and fun the next, you never knew how the mood would take him. He preferred boys to girls. He played chess with the boys and praised their work. Girls were objects of ridicule and he constantly made fun of us. Once he made a girl walk around the classroom with her dress pulled up to show everyone her knickers. This was his 'fun' mode, as it was when he asked girls to take off their vests and run around topless at the bottom of the school field.

When Mr. K ran shaming sessions my heart sank. It was his time to teach us a lesson, using a particular girl as his 'instrument'. We were held in his mesmeric spell, day in, day out – a terrifying suspense of violence or eroticism. Would today be a smacking day or a groping day? One never knew. Either way it would always humiliate and could also hurt.

As one of his 'instruments' I was often involved. I lost count of the number of times I was put over Mr. K's knee in front of my schoolmates and either smacked, tickled or groped in full view. My desk was positioned close by and he could grab me at will. If he were in a playful mood he would molest me by tickling and feeling inside my underwear whilst holding me still. I still remember the putrid smell of his armpits as he pressed me close to his side whilst pushing his hands relentlessly across my body. If I wriggled away he would get rough, so I tried to comply. When he released me from his grip, I returned to my seat, my face burning scarlet, sensations coursing through my body that I didn't understand.

Sometimes I made eye contact with my friend Lizzie who looked nervous, reassuring her I was fine. But mostly I kept my head and eyes down until the feelings subsided and the moment had passed. My ears burned the most, and a high-pitched ringing pierced my brain. But honestly, I preferred the groping to the smacking. Groping meant that I was Mr. K's favourite for the day. The smacking had anger behind it. It frightened me more. It meant I was in trouble, that I had done something to upset him. Logic told me to be good. Top marks good. I thought that being co-operative, getting good grades, being affable, would keep me out of trouble. I *wanted* to be his favourite.

Mr. K exploited this desire. He encouraged me to stay behind after lessons to have 'little chats', all of which took place at the entrance to the girls' toilets. He engaged me in a confusing dialogue that made me yearn for his approval. He talked about the other girls in my class, the way they behaved, what he thought of them, how I compared to them, what they did right, what I did wrong. He compared my work to the boys' and constantly reminded me of the imminent parents' evening when he would give his report. He encouraged me to get close to him, to ask him for hugs, to 'seek his attention'. Yet I left feeling desperately ashamed, a wretchedness that gnawed away inside as I took the long walk home alone. I felt that I would never be good enough.

By the time parents' evening arrived I was in a state of high anxiety, waiting desperately for the sound of my parents' car to pull into the drive. When they finally arrived home they looked concerned and asked to me to sit down so we could talk.

'Mr. K is concerned about your behaviour', they said.

'Your marks are good but he said you have been trying to seek his attention in a way that's not appropriate for an eight-year-old girl. He said that you've been making advances towards him – asking for his affection. What do you think he is talking about?' My jaw dropped. I couldn't believe it.

My parents looked at me in a way that I knew was a potential 'good hiding' situation if I wasn't careful.

'It isn't like that!' I said.

'Well what do you think he means?' It seemed that my parents believed him.

'I don't know what he means', I said, hanging my head in shame.

I was floored. Mr. K had played his trump card.

No matter how hard I tried after that, in my mind I was already beaten. I became obsessed with trying to be better, the best, perfect, desperately trying to get things under control. I trace my eating disorders back to this time, my overachieving, throwing myself into schoolwork, trying always to be top. If there were any way of putting pressure on myself I would find it, even to the point of stopping myself from peeing. My mother found me one day, lying on the bathroom floor, clinging to the radiator, writhing in pain. I'd created an infection, which meant I couldn't pee at all. I felt powerless.

Once, after a particularly violent episode in the classroom which involved one of my friends, I remember a conversation with her and another kid. One of them said, 'There is nothing we can do now, no one would believe us. But one day', she said, 'one day we will be adults and then we will do something.'

For now, daydreaming was the only escape. I spent my last two years of junior school retreating to a fantasy world in my head using a vivid imagination. Every story I wrote ended with me heralded for heroic behaviour, the reward always coming in the shape of a pretty dress. I longed for luxury, resenting the clothes that were handed down from Mum's friends. I created a dream world, transporting myself to a time in the future when a boy who understood my struggles would appear and we would run away together. In my fairy-tale mind I was Cinderella, Snow White and the Sleeping Beauty. But when it came to the real business of casting the final-year pantomime I was given a lead part, not as the princess of my dreams but as the wicked witch. I wanted to scream and cry as they dressed me up in black and green and painted my face to look as ugly as possible. I wasn't fooling anyone, including myself. Deep inside I knew I was already scarred.

I arrived at senior school in September 1979, a year marked by the start of the Thatcher administration. Derby School, once a grammar school, now a comprehensive, drew its pupils partly from the leafy suburbs and partly from the inner city. Geographically I sat somewhere in the middle, living neither in pretty, affluent Littleover, nor in terraced, ethnic Normanton, but in relatively drab Sunnyhill which was the first bus stop on the route that didn't qualify for the free bus pass. I made a three-mile walk up streets and alleys before a final stretch across some fields with horses in them.

Academically I could keep up. Socially I was fragile, with 'bully me' invisibly written on my forehead. Trying to be the best at everything attracted attention but was usually mistaken for arrogance. I wasn't robust enough for peer-group politics, so one false move and I faced hostility, whispering, being laughed at, rejected. I sunk fast and wept for hours before school, sobbing to the Radio 1 breakfast show as I lay in bed, wishing the day was already over. I often pleaded with my parents not to make me go to school, one day collapsing in a heap of tears outside our front door, the bristles of the doormat scratching my knees as I begged them through the glass: 'Please don't make me go'.

In the classroom I was lonely and miserable. The girls made fun of me at every opportunity, and I couldn't handle it. I wandered the school playing fields at breaks, avoiding the other children as best I could. At home I fainted at the breakfast table, my head landing in the butter before I collapsed on the floor. When my mother took me to the doctor he diagnosed depression but offered no solution. It was my first rock bottom.

Eventually it was the relentless focus on schoolwork that paid off when we were streamed by our abilities. The following school year started with the excitement of being in the top class, which spurred me on. I pushed myself harder for even better results. Tired of being bullied by my father, my teacher, my friends, I dyed my hair in different colours, wore make up, and created an image that said 'I don't care', 'I'm different', 'You don't know what you're dealing with'. I sensed a change in the way I was regarded. It made me feel in control, like I had turned things around. I had found an identity that seemed to fit.

I found further release at our local swimming pool where my father would take us most Saturday afternoons. From the moment I walked through the sliding doors I was hooked. The hit of warm air mixed with the smell of chlorine was intoxicating. That was even before I had stepped through the brightly coloured footbath and into the echoing spaciousness of the pool itself, with its diving area set back grandly, springboards and high boards calling all champions and dismissing all cowards by their towering presence alone.

One day a friend encouraged me to take diving lessons with her. After a six-week course I was asked to join the junior team. My love of water was combined with the adrenaline rush of flying through the air. And there truly was no greater satisfaction than a perfect dive when I hit the water in a straight line, making an air bubble with my hands to cushion the impact and take down the entire splash. In this moment of perfection, as I plunged deep into the water, the sound of silence was blissful. These were the moments I lived for, where my life went into slo-mo and the world stopped turning. All of my problems in life, the pressures, the anxiety, the peer politics, the shouting, the arguing, the fighting, the punishments, school, everything, just faded away. I was an extraordinary mermaid, slowly gliding to the bottom of the pool, and then effortlessly pushing myself up towards the surface. The lights above would grow closer until I broke through the surface, and when I did all of the noises of real life were there waiting for me, a deafening reminder that nothing had changed. Here was life with all its challenges, marked by the harsh sounds of the attendants' whistles, the shouts of the swimmers as they called to each other, the spectators in the gallery. Then I would turn to look at my coach to see the approval on his face, or not, depending on how I had performed. I was compelled to take another dive. It was exhilarating.

As the years progressed so did my diving. I mastered harder dives and competed at national level, sometimes winning trophies and medals. Training was rigorous and involved at least four sessions a week with the team. One evening our training night was relaxed. My friend Nigel, a brilliant diver, was in a good mood, messing about between dives. He was singing Eddie Grant's 'I Don't Wanna Dance', jumping off the side and seeing how many twists he could do before hitting the water. Things changed in a second when he took an extra large leap, singing at the top of his voice, and twisted three times before landing – not in the water but on concrete. With his head.

Nigel slumped lifelessly into the water and floated beneath the surface. I hoped he might still be joking around, pretending to be unconscious. But if he wasn't, I needed to save him. Hedging my bets, I leaped into the pool, shouting, 'I'll save you, Nigel!' As soon as I touched his body I knew – and held him in my arms while treading water. His head was on my shoulder, his eyeballs rolled into the back of his head and saliva dribbled from his mouth.

Our coach dragged him onto the poolside. He gave mouth to mouth and Nigel was sick, his eyes still rolling weirdly into the back of head, his strong body now uncannily limp. We were taken to the changing rooms and the ambulance came. I shook uncontrollably, unable to get dressed as the paramedics pushed Nigel's stretcher through the sliding doors, his departure marked by the wail of a siren that penetrated the gloomy silence as we all went home. That night I couldn't sleep. The image of Nigel's face close to mine as I'd held him in the water, burned into my mind's eye. It was a long night but the morning brought good news. Although he had fractured his skull and there was internal bleeding he was going to live. In time Nigel made a full recovery, but he never dived again. A few months later I received a beautifully wrapped present and a card from him that said, *Thank you for saving my life*.

For a while my sports career progressed in leaps and bounds. I had a good relationship with my coach, who collected me from school and took me training, one to one. I could talk to him about almost anything, and he made me laugh. He believed in me. He saw my potential and then patiently worked with me step by step. I won the county championships and we went into winter training, optimistic for the following season. I took on bigger dives that needed a crash jacket as I spun through several somersaults, sometimes missing my entry and crashing hard on the water's surface. In moments like these the image of Nigel's face would reappear. I'm not sure that it ever entirely left.

One evening, as I stood backwards on the springboard, preparing to dive, my mind went completely blank. My stomach flipped over and I fell into the water. I went back to the board and tried again. The same thing happened. I couldn't do it. Coach told me to call it a night and we'd resume tomorrow, but when tomorrow came my thoughts were even more disconnected. The same thing happened the following night. And again, the night after that... Within a fortnight, five years of dedicated work came to an end. It scared me that something I was so good at could disappear overnight. My coach was upset. He tried not to show it but his disappointment rushed over both of us. I was devastated. Just like Nigel's, my diving dream was over.

At home, life was as stressful as ever. My father, keen to take his religious career beyond teaching, locked himself away in our caravan on the front drive, rattling away at his typewriter for hours, bringing out a series of analytical Christian books. His writing was squeezed between his full-time teaching job and his religious studies at theological college in Lincoln where he was training to become a priest. After five years he was ordained into the Church of England. He then worked as a non-stipendiary priest in a community church set on an impoverished estate while he continued as a full-time teacher and a part-time author.

Coming from a religious family already made me different from most of my school friends. Their families passed through a church door for weddings and funerals rather than a regular spiritual practice. But to become a 'vicar's daughter' introduced a new stigma, a certain expectation. I participated in church activities – dance groups, choir and youth club. I prayed every day. I practised the Christian faith. When the congregation sang with guitars and drums, creating an uplifting rhythm, I felt connected with myself, with others, with my spirit. But one day my parents became embroiled in an argument with the vicar and his wife, both of whom suddenly wanted them to leave the church. It was never clear to me what the issue was, and my parents put up a long and drawn-out fight to stay. My mother was often in tears when I came home from school. I didn't get it.

One evening Mum came off the phone, shouting and screaming at my father, pushing him and pulling him around. My stomach churned into knots of dreadful anxiety. What could have happened? What had he done? My father called for a doctor who sedated her, and while my mother slept he told me she'd had nervous breakdown. Mum and Dad stopped going to church after this, and I lost my faith in a religion where people would treat each other in such a way. What couldn't be resolved with prayer? Then, just when it seemed things couldn't get much worse, my father came home after a disciplinary incident in his classroom. He was suspended, pending a tribunal, which never took place because he retired from teaching.

Our relationship deteriorated even more. Once he was so angry he pushed me downstairs and threw me out of the house, telling me never to come back. I welcomed the invitation and felt disappointed when he pulled up alongside me in the car, angrily demanding 'Get in!' Now I can see how stressed Dad was, wrestling with his faith, trying to pick up the pieces from his and Mum's breakdowns, struggling to make ends meet financially. At the time I was wrapped up in all of it, emotionally bearing the brunt of it and feeling responsible, as I always had.

Without the regular escape of diving, I immersed myself in friendships, underscored by our shared love of music and dancing. It was the 1980s and we rode the new wave of electronic music, a flamboyant expression of liberated youth. I was drawn towards moody bands who sang of angst and unrequited love. Soft Cell's 'Tainted Love' captivated me, and I played Marc Almond's songs over and over, absorbing myself

14

in his melancholic lyrics: *They say home is where the heart is, but you know home is where the hurt is*[2], and, *I'm skilled at the art of falling apart*[3]. Not just every word, I knew every breath, and every note. I pored over *Smash Hits* and read about the Batcave and Heaven nightclubs in London which he frequented, along with all the big bands of that time: Culture Club, Visage, Spandau Ballet, Duran Duran... One day I would move to London and be part of that scene. I just knew.

Fiona was my best friend. After being together all day at school we would spend all evening on the phone. We sat together in class, we went out together at weekends. On Saturday night we dressed up and met the rest of the gang. I was creative with my fashion sense, watching the magazines carefully before taking the next step in outrageousness, sometimes going as far as wearing dustbin liners with studded belts and many earrings. Down town I would lose myself on the dance floor, my heart uplifted by the beat of the music. *Ain't nobody, loves me better, makes me feel good, makes me feel this way*[4]. Chaka Khan was right. I adored my friends, each and every one, as I danced around them, all of us high on the spirit of youth.

A sixth-form field trip to Scarborough was the highlight of our school year – a week away with your best friends and the super-cool teachers. One night, the girls were in my room and I was the entertainment. As I fooled about, laughing and kicking, I felt my knee pop, and when I looked down my kneecap wasn't there. It had slid to the back of my leg, making it look, oddly, as if my leg was on backwards. I screamed. Fiona screamed. Everyone screamed. I fell onto the bed in excruciating pain and a schoolteacher came in to deal with the chaos. It took over an hour before a doctor came and another before an ambulance arrived. The girls tried to keep up my spirits by singing 'Tainted Love' a hundred times, telling stories and cracking jokes, but when the ambulance eventually appeared I was delirious. Somewhere along the line I passed out, and when I woke up in the ambulance, my knee was back in place. I spent the rest of the trip on my own in the guesthouse, depressed and lonely, smoking cigarettes and looking forward to the evening when we could go to the pub. My friends got me through that experience.

And then there were boys.

When I first heard mention of girls having boyfriends I was petrified. When a boy from school delivered a Valentine card to my house I spent the rest of the evening vomiting in the toilet. I don't even know why I was scared; I was just rigid with fear and so ashamed. I truly wanted the ground to open up and swallow me. My first date was the same. A boy in my class who looked like a mix between Marc Almond, David Sylvian from Japan, and Robert Smith from The Cure, asked me out to see *Merry Christmas Mr Lawrence* on a Saturday night. I was so self-conscious all evening that I couldn't focus on the film for a second. Only its haunting soundtrack played in my head as we made our way home in awkward silence.

Alcohol was my saving grace. With alcohol everything became incredibly easy. Or, I should say, with alcohol I became incredibly easy. The desire to be loved, to be wanted and to be validated ran so strongly within me that I found it easy to satisfy the desires in others. I would do anything, and ironically, for all the fear at first, sex became my powerful ally. It was intense. It was seductive. And so was I.

My first boyfriend was a schoolmate whom I had known for years, and I trusted him. We tried to have sex a few times but we both lacked technique and my virginity remained stubbornly intact, despite our best efforts. He went out with another girl in our class and I hid my disappointment beneath an air of bravado and indifference. When I was sixteen I met an older boy who worked as an electrician and part-time model. Toddy took my virginity for real after we 'broke into' his friend's empty house in a part of town that I didn't know. He persuaded me to climb through a small kitchen window, and I delicately negotiated stacks of dirty pots and pans next to overflowing ashtrays as I jumped off the draining board and onto a scummy kitchen floor. After I'd let Toddy in through the backdoor he said we should keep the house dark so we wouldn't alert the neighbours. I was glad. The place was a mess and it smelt nasty. We went upstairs and found a bedroom. We lay down on the bed. My moment had arrived.

Kissing Toddy was really good, and the excitement I felt in the hands of someone who knew what they were doing was electric. There was no feeling like it. Any question over my virginity was certainly resolved at the point of penetration, a burning shaft that stole my passion and replaced it with pain. My discomfort went unnoticed to my lover who was greedily enjoying his moment in a rapturous succession of thrusts and shouts. Before too long it was over, and we lay and chatted for ages, our closeness cemented by our intimate exchange. We had little in common other than our shared chemistry, and, after a succession of similar evenings, sexual encounters snatched in public car parks and local playing fields, we called it a day.

My next boyfriend was already at university while I was still at school. He seemed to really like me but he gave me an infection the first time we slept together. I had to skip classes to go to the clinic on my own, and I couldn't resolve being with him after having my legs up in stirrups and a strong dose of antibiotics that made me feel sick. I was depressed that week, and lonely, having to hide the situation from my mother and most of my friends. And then there was a boyfriend who didn't tell me he might be gay, pushing and pulling me back and forth before finally coming out. *No, I'm not happy for you!* I was disillusioned with it all.

And then finally. There he was. Russell. My first love. Better than anyone I could have imagined. A star athlete who had won a scholarship to a public school. He was tall, with a

17

sprinter's build, shockingly good looking, and he even wore eyeliner and spiked his hair. We met at a party that Fiona and her boyfriend took me to. I didn't know it was a set-up. We were introduced: me, the ex-diver, him, the fastest runner of his age in the country. We recognised something of ourselves in each other. He had lost his younger sister to cancer ten years before, since when he had retreated inside himself, become shy and withdrawn from people. When I told him about my life, he seemed to understand. He was a soul mate. We became close and a loyal and precious relationship started to flourish. After three months my friends started asking if we had slept together. We hadn't. It was enough just being with each other, hanging out, kissing, holding hands, listening to music, watching him train or compete at the track, riding on rollercoasters at the theme park, anything... But eventually we found the courage and it happened. It was lovely of course. But I struggled after that.

I felt vulnerable and became insecure, clinging to him and feeling bereft when we were apart. He was completely devoted to me, never a flirt. His mother called me her future daughter-in-law. But it was never enough. I would cry myself to sleep at the thought of him wanting someone else, or I would obsess over his ex-girlfriends who were few and in no way significant. Deep down I was overwhelmed with this love yet petrified of becoming 'trapped' so I created arguments about his lack of love for me. Love felt hard. It didn't solve anything. It didn't stop the confusion, the pain, the hurting. If anything it created more. There was more to lose. I never felt good enough. I would lose him. I would lose everything. I knew I would.

The pressure to do well at school was also on, with a university place at stake. I smoked cigarettes and drank to numb my feelings, but this led to mood swings and it didn't help. I revised furiously for my mock A-level exams, diligently sitting at home with timetables and books, learning each literary text and every historical date off by heart. But when I went into the first exam, I broke down in tears. Even though I knew the answer to every question on the paper, I couldn't write. I couldn't function. The teacher took me outside. I sobbed uncontrollably until they called my mother to take me home. I couldn't articulate *what* was wrong; I just knew there was *something* wrong. Life scared me so much, and no one anywhere could help. Not Russell, not his parents, not my parents, not my friends. Everyone had his or her life, and mine was rubbish. I was a failure. The same feeling of hopelessness from when I was nine engulfed me. *What was the point?*

Such were the thoughts that made me reach for a bottle of spirit and a bottle of strong painkillers. What did I care if I lived or died? What did anyone care? As my consciousness slipped away I fell into a nightmarish sleep, weighed down by a desperate feeling of despair. I woke up some hours later to the sound of Mum knocking on my bedroom door. I was oddly relieved. I told her what I had done and she looked at me blankly. She was at a loss. The next day she took me to the doctor who prescribed anti-depressants and a week off school because he was at a loss too. My overdose was a cry for help. What I needed was an intervention, someone to guide me onto a road of recovery and healing.

The closest I came was a talk with the head of year. I asked him if he could help me get my own place, somewhere quiet, where I could focus. He said it was possible but instead suggested that if I kept my head down at home for just a short while longer, I would soon be free. He inspired me. He gave me a vision of what was possible. A fresh departure. The next day I woke up, flushed the meds down the toilet, went to the library, stuck my head in a book and shut out everything around me. I ignored anything that could distract me, the gossip, the messing about in the classroom, the problems and arguments at home. Everything. I managed to take control. And when the day of the exam results arrived, I surpassed most people in my year. My escape route was secured.

That summer unfolded like a dream. I worked and put money in the bank. Russell and I went to Ibiza and danced at the Ku Club Tropicana, just like George Michael. I fell in love with the Mediterranean, its deep blue warmth and its soft white-sand beaches. We dived off boats and swam in its magical light. Russell competed for the England team while his mum and I screamed encouragement from the stands in our desperate, often hysterical desire for him to cross the finish line first. He often did.

Every day was amazing, and I never wanted it to end, ignoring the sense of approaching doom that gnawed away in the pit of my stomach when I thought about us parting for our respective universities. Even my driving test coincided with an extraordinary event when a deceased parishioner left his car to my father, a pale blue vintage Triumph Herald. To my complete amazement Dad said it was mine if I passed my test. Of course I passed! Getting a set of keys to my own car was an unimagined freedom. Nothing could hold me back now. The Derby ring road could have been Highway 1 at the Big Sur. I was Penelope Pitstop with her fabulous make-up mirror and designer ashtray, my long hair blowing in the breeze. We loaded up the car when it was time to leave, Russell joining me for the five-hour journey. My parents and brothers waved me off from the driveway. Finally I was leaving home.

The stakes raised tenfold as I drove myself into the academic and political environment of Lancaster University. After I'd checked into the Halls of Residence and located my room, I drove Russell to the train station. We said our tearful goodbyes on the platform, promising to see each other soon. Then I set off in the wrong direction going for miles before I realized my mistake. A fog descended and I could hardly see the road ahead as I veered round corners, tears streaming down my face. When

I finally made it back to my room, I played over and over my feelings of abandonment with every spin of The Communards' 'Don't Leave Me This Way'. This was how love felt. This was my fairy-tale love story. Loss, separation and being alone. I cried myself to sleep that night, longing once again for my happily ever after. Life felt like hell sometimes. But within that hell something else had stirred.

The seed of my fighting spirit, the desire to get out of hell, was born.

Chapter Two

Hunger

*When hell changes into the realm of hungry spirits, that
is no longer the true form of hell.*
The True Aspect of All Phenomena[1]

Hunger. When desires are never satisfied and nothing is enough.
A constant craving. The condition of being unfulfilled. Not to
be confused with starvation, hunger takes hold within even the
wealthiest of societies, sometimes at stratospheric levels. Super
yachts are one example. Cosmetic surgery is another.

For me, hunger manifested in addiction. I used things to
fix the way I felt about myself. Except that the 'fixes', which
were designed to soothe and numb my pain, eventually became
destructive and self-defeating. From the age of five, when I got
hooked on fantasy, right through to my late thirties when I
used sex, drugs, money and love for the same reason, *never
being enough* was well-worn ground. If I tried to control one
addiction, another would take its place. Constant craving. This
was my disease.

University life provided superbly fertile soil. As I emerged
from a brief but heavy sleep on my first college morning, I was
already in the grip of an emotional hangover. Waking up to a
feeling of dread was fairly normal. That familiar sinking feeling
in the pit of my stomach had been firmly established during

my primary school days. Education equalled anxiety. But today, my first morning at college, the dread held an unfamiliar and ominous quality. Today I was really 'out there.'

Noises in the corridor, slamming doors, voices I didn't recognise… There was only so long before I would have to open my door. At some point I would need to pee. I held it as long as possible, that secret power I'd been working on since I was eight. I would go out there when I was ready, not when my bladder dictated. I turned back to the smacked-out feeling in my head and my puffy, tear-stained eyes. How I longed for Russell right now. My best friend. My rock. I wanted to phone him. I would have to find a phone. In the meantime, I needed to find enough strength to face the world outside my room.

After a cigarette and a cup of coffee I ventured out. A group of girls sat in the kitchen around the table with, absurdly, a canoe on top of it. It was a small kitchen and a fairly large canoe, each with the capacity to seat around four people. The canoe actually stretched out of the kitchen and into an adjoining seating area. The girls were talking animatedly between themselves. My appearance at the kitchen door made them stop mid-sentence. One of them jumped up and introduced herself.

'Hi, I'm Rachel', she said. 'We're just trying to work out what to do with this boat. What's your name?'

'I'm Ruth', I said, smiling. 'How did it get here?'

'Some guys got drunk and thought it would be really funny to leave it in a freshers' kitchen.'

'Wankers', I said. The girls laughed.

'Are you a first year?' Rachel asked me.

'Yes, of course.'

'Are you 18?'

'Yes.'

'We all thought you were a mature student when you arrived yesterday. You looked really confident. Like you knew what you're doing.'

'Nothing could be further from the truth.' I laughed. 'But thanks for the vote of confidence.'

As I made my introductions to the rest of my housemates, all fourteen of them, it was clear that I had experienced the least sheltered upbringing of all. However dreadful I may have felt, my low self-esteem was not apparent to them. As I dragged on another cigarette before breakfast the smoke provided a thin screen of confidence.

'We're going on a bar crawl tonight', Rachel said. 'Are you in?'

'Sure, why not.'

And so we were off.

I had opted for an Arts degree, English and Theatre; my favourite subjects. At school the Arts had provided a welcome escape to places created by people I considered more talented than myself: musicians, artists, actors and writers who skilfully forged exciting new worlds into which I could project my fantasies. Now, as an undergraduate within an academic environment, it wasn't the studies that fazed me; rather it was the sense of community that I found overwhelming.

In halls my friends were law and economics students, keen to play pool while drinking endlessly in the various campus bars. Afterwards we would sit around our communal kitchen until the early hours, talking and joking, a mounting pile of dirty dishes overflowing from the sink. Most were from the Home Counties, a new conservatism propelling them towards their future careers in banking and business. On the theatre course my friends were arty and political, throwing themselves into productions that involved long rehearsals followed by even longer discussions in the bar, or house parties and dancing to unwind. These friends, who also came from comfortable homes, took on 'issues' by joining rallies and marches at weekends. For a while I was unsure where I fitted, and was torn, running madly between two very different scenes.

Even harder was balancing college life with seeing Russell at weekends, either at my place or his. I enjoyed the journey between, a train ride across the Pennines, when I would read and listen to music on my Walkman: Kate Bush *Hounds of Love*, or U2 *The Joshua Tree*. *And I still haven't found what I'm looking for...*[2]

And I hadn't.

On one hand, I loved Russell with all my heart. More than that, I needed him. Yet, although I longed for him when we were apart, I found his life in Leeds awkward and uncomfortable. I couldn't relate to his college friends, who were all sports students. Maybe it was just one scene too many or maybe we truly had little in common. When Russell visited me I found it just as tricky trying to bring him into my world. As much as I fought it, I knew we were growing apart. While Russell's drama was unfolding on the running track, with early morning training sessions and a healthy lifestyle to support his Olympic aspirations, my dramatic goals were pulling me in a very different direction. The theatre studio on campus was a state-of-the-art facility, vast in scale and full of the latest technology. It housed an unending programme of intense productions to which we had unlimited access. The pressures of acting and directing, a deep sense of self-absorption – I gravitated to all of this. And the stakes were high.

The theatre department was an exclusive clique, with unspoken rules of acceptance and an unforgiving spirit of perfection. To win respect not only relied on talent but on being in favour with the right lecturers who cast the productions and awarded the grades. For a visiting lecturer who came from a highly acclaimed physical theatre company in London I observed my peers do anything to be in his favour, including performing naked, or eating newspaper then vomiting it up on stage. With my athletic background, physical theatre should have been my forte – but I cowered from him.

In spite of this, however, I did get involved and I did make friends. I was part of the stage crew for a large production of *Hamlet* which featured all the rising stars. During rehearsals, as we crouched excitedly in the wings, my friend Bella described the various personalities, giving me the low-down on the group dynamics that were clearly emerging. A choreographer called Sara (two years ahead of me) assisted the lecturer who was in charge of the production. I longed to be like her and was astonished when she offered her friendship later that year. This creative environment seduced me. I needed to be part of it, even if I felt unworthy of being included.

The turning point came when one of the senior lecturers let me assistant direct on her production of Shakespeare's *As You Like It*. It was my moment to step into the limelight and I rose to the task in the same way I would have approached a diving board in my teens, with single-minded determination. I knew what I needed to do, and I had one chance to get it right.

All at once, there I was, seated beside the head of department as the auditions for the largest production of the year took place. Those once-distant students who had captured my imagination a year earlier, as I'd watched their performances from the sidelines, were now in very close range. Some were extraordinarily beautiful, others talented in the extreme. I could see they had questions, 'Who is she?' 'What is she doing here?' I was polite, respectful, not pushy, I kept holding onto the belief that I knew how to do this. I knew how to direct. And when it came to conducting my first rehearsal alone with the two lead actors, I utilised the long experience of handling my father's volatile personality. They were easy in comparison and went away from the session feeling happy and uplifted. The leading man, Orlando, who had visibly doubted me at first, seemed to warm to me the most. With him on side I knew I would be OK.

After a few more rehearsals I gained everyone's trust and the process ran more smoothly than I ever could have wished. I had become part of the group to which I aspired. In fact, as the show neared production week, I seemed to have gained more kudos than the director herself.

I confided in my friend Bella.

'Ride the wave of success', she reassured me.

'I can't enjoy it', I said. 'I feel that it will crash at any moment.'

'*All the world's a stage, And all the men and women merely players*', she said mischievously, quoting a central line from the play. She was right of course. We were all simply playing our part.

But what was my part? I kept asking myself. *Who was I supposed to be?* Success, it seemed, caused as much stress as failure, simply because of the fear of not being able to keep up the act. I wasn't able to articulate this gnawing feeling of insecurity to Russell. Instead, the fear would seep out in nervous, irritable moods which created tension when we were together. I was between a rock and a hard place. And from this unbearably uncomfortable place I made a move.

I broke off my relationship with him.

I was led not by a rational decision about what would be good for me, but from a compulsion that was rooted in addiction. There wasn't enough because *I* wasn't enough. It was going to end at some point anyway, I thought, so I might as well take things into my own hands.

Russell, heartbroken, pleaded with me to reconsider, suggesting ways that we could work it out. His mum tried to talk to me. His dad was devastated. It was the worst thing I could have done and I felt terrible. From the moment I had first slept with Russell I hadn't felt good enough for him, and now I had proved it. Inside I shut down, disconnecting myself from feelings that were too wretched to acknowledge.

Sex was the drug that I used to survive, throwing myself at Orlando at the last night party of *As You Like It,* to which he responded with flattering enthusiasm. I lost myself in a dopamine high from which I refused to come down. We were rarely out of bed, and even on campus we found hidden locations to sustain our ecstasy, acting out our sexuality like extraordinary porn stars. There could never be enough of this, our bodies visibly steaming in the throes of passion, my vagina sore from day upon night of endless fucking. Now I was validated. Now I had found my place centre stage. And yet, although Orlando devoted himself to me completely, I began to struggle again. Despite the comfort of sex and a new love, I craved something more.

Food. If I couldn't control my feelings, I could at least create a distraction from them. Starvation offered a perfect solution. Within a department of drama students who were required to look a certain way, in the silent competition for whose Levi's hung most blithely from under-nourished bones, I often won. I ate as little as humanly possible, numbing my appetite with an endless stream of cigarettes. I would be sexy and skinny. It would help oil the machine.

And drugs. With Orlando I switched from alcohol to cannabis. I was happy stoned, easily satisfied, curled up in front of the fire with a joint and a cup of tea, holding soul-searching debates with my friends. Sara and I would solve the world's problems, and occasionally our own, over a pot of English Breakfast and a packet of Jaffa Cakes. And when her boyfriend Tony visited from London, Orlando and I would play cards with them, enjoying easy banter as joints were passed around into the early hours. It was amazing how long we could make drugs last. On more than one occasion Bella and I misplaced the last nugget of gear in our hazy high only to search for it everywhere the following day. Once we found it inside the vacuum cleaner, and I'm sure we frequently smoked something that had fallen from the bottom of Orlando's shoe.

My smoking escalated when I made friends with a guy who used very strong grass. We worked on a project which I directed and he performed: *Krapp's Last Tape*. We spent most of our rehearsal time getting high. One night I experienced falling into a psychedelic tunnel, sucked into a terrifying feeling of being trapped. I couldn't speak and numbly made my way home, hardly recognising the streets along the way. I was so relieved when I finally turned the key in my front door. Yet even though the experience was awful it left me wanting to do it again. I wanted to beat the feeling of powerlessness and give into it all at the same time.

I earned money by working for a kissogram agency, which involved dressing up in 'sexy underwear' beneath a long coat, then turning up at someone's birthday party or other social event and surprising them (coat now off) by reading a poem about the unsuspecting victim. 'Surprise, surprise, I bet you didn't expect this, well your friends have asked me to come along and give you a birthday kiss!' I would declare in some of the most unexpected places, from the meat counter of a supermarket in Kendal, to a Kwik Fit garage on Carnforth industrial estate, and even on the boardroom table at a local shipping company's annual general meeting. One chaste peck on the cheek at the end and I was out of there, cash rich and back to the sanctuary of my housemates and a joint in front of the fire.

It was deceptive. The evenings of hilarity with Sara, Tony and Orlando were great. The rest of the time what looked good from the outside was not necessarily so. Internally I struggled to keep a hold on my thoughts, often spinning into a secret well of paranoia and doubt. Even with my housemates I would find myself caught in an internal monologue of self-loathing while I projected laid-back insouciance. This is how it was: a succession of highs and lows. The highs were usually public, and sometimes on a stage, usually under a spotlight, whereas the lows were hidden from view, occasionally seen by a close friend when the pressure became too much and I crashed. I could pick myself up and put things together, performing well in my studies and graduating with high honours, but it was love where I would fail.

As my relationship with Orlando ran its course sex became a contradiction. Although I reached for it to feel better, I would get lost in the intensity of it, so that it felt overwhelming and eventually left me feeling worse. Sometimes I would shut down completely, insisting on us being friends instead of lovers. Sometimes I had sex with other people behind Orlando's back, and felt horribly guilty. Yet I blamed the relationship, concluding that love with the right person must feel better than this.

Intrigued by several lesbians in the department who were confident of their sexual preference, I wondered if I too might be gay. I grew close to a female friend who had already left college and worked as a journalist in the city nearby. She stayed with Orlando and me as she was preparing to leave the country to join her girlfriend in Spain and the chemistry between us developed rapidly. On her last night Orlando was out of town. We ate out, sharing a bottle of wine over witty conversation, our eyes locked in a sparkling dance of mutual attraction. When we got back to the house we were buzzing from a compelling mixture of alcohol and sexual energy. Yet, when my friend asked if she could sleep in my bed I still thought we were just friends. A normal girls sleep over. Nothing would happen.

At first we just lay there, not even touching. The lights were out. She didn't move. Neither did I. But inside I was exploding, my heart beating so loud I was sure she could hear it. After a lifetime, it seemed, we edged our way closer. One breath at a time. One inch at a time. It took forever. Time stood still. And when we met, our hands gently touched. Even more moments of even more lifetimes before the tension finally eased. Yes, this was for real. The energetic gears shifted, providing relief on one hand, yet a further surge of anticipation on the other as the acknowledgement of mutual desire brought forth fresh expectations. I was about to have sex with a woman. And when I did, it blew my mind.

Maybe the forbidden nature of this sapphic experience intensified the excitement. For a short while I fell into what I thought was the deepest love I had ever known. I thought of this woman day and night, counting the minutes until I would see her again. I longed to be close to her, I yearned for her, replaying over and over a mix-tape she had made, living and breathing the words of every song, from Marvin Gaye's 'Let's Get It On' to John Martyn's 'If You Ever'.

When she left the country to be with her girlfriend, my heart was ripped from my chest. A familiar feeling, this agonising love, but I see now that it wasn't love at all. It was another dimension of my addiction, another way to act out. I confused intensity with intimacy, a characteristic of love addiction that was to develop in the years to come. Intensity had marked this whole experience, from its momentary yet illusory high until it threw me to the floor. Opening the door to my bisexuality didn't provide any answers, just a whole heap more questions. I was back in the solitary confinement of my childhood bedroom, sobbing alone, hugging my knees and wanting to escape to a place far away. Which is exactly what I decided to do.

In the absence of any career ambitions and in the stark light of my flailing relationship with Orlando it was the lure of sun, sea and a 'place far away' that prompted me to apply for jobs in the tourist industry. I was posted to Mallorca, and tasked with meeting holidaymakers off their charter flights and selling them excursions from their hotel. I hated every moment of it. After a week I was ready to come home.

On my day off I drove across the island to see the one decent friend I'd made in the short time we'd been there. She had been relocated to a different resort. It was a beautiful drive in dappled sunlight, the bright azure Mediterranean on one side and terraces of olive trees on the other. While I waited at her hotel I chatted to its head of entertainments, and within half an hour they had offered me a job as an entertainer. I celebrated with a swim in the hotel pool, the sea glittering in the distance, my heart lifting with every stroke. The job was a dream and I led an enviable life – suntanned, on permanent holiday, and being paid for it. Even on my days off, the dream continued. I would find a secluded cove along the coast and swim in its warm waters, then join the locals and relax with a bunch of new friends.

But my longing for love and the wounds of heartbreak ached painfully beneath the surface. I drank vodka from morning to night, which from the first sip washed over the pain like a clear anaesthetic, giving me clarity and confidence. It helped me play the part of the attractive athlete skipping around the pool in my swimming costume by day, and the humourous entertainer by night as I compèred shows in the auditorium. I still searched for love, still sought a person to relate to, a like-minded soul who would understand me. Instead I found the affection of another entertainer who slept around. I stuck with him for a short while, tolerating his lack of commitment, and we went as far as looking for winter work in Tenerife. After a few days, we had a fight that ended when I hit him in self-defence and broke my finger. After forty-eight hours of Spanish clinics and miserable self-reflection, I called Orlando who had moved to London and flew home to be with him.

Poor Orlando. There he was, waiting for me for at the airport, hurt after the way I had left him but willing to forgive. Even now Orlando offered partnership and longevity. I pondered this in the light of my own lack of direction and purpose as, arm in a sling, I limped back into his life. Once again I had the opportunity to settle down with a man who cared for me, but within days I knew I couldn't stay. I craved excitement, intensity and drama, all of which would manifest in three significant relationships, all with men called Paul.

Paul W was the first. He had been a fellow classmate at University, and from the start he had held my attention. Fresh from marching for his rights at Gay Pride during the unlikely and unprecedented alliance between the Miners Union and the Gay movement, Paul W arrived from London – out, loud and very proud. He impressed me with his bold stance on HIV issues, writing and directing a play called *10 Days,* the time it then took to get back your HIV blood test results. He was great fun to be with and over the years at college we'd become close friends, sharing a deep connection, bonded by our mutual struggle to hide low self-esteem behind our popular and outspoken facades.

When I moved to London, with my broken hand and ragged heart, Paul was there, now opening a doorway to the heady world of narcotics. The underground dance scene was raving, and although the Batcave of my teenage dreams was over, on the way to meet Paul on my very first day in London, who should be standing right in front of me in the Covent Garden General Store but Marc Almond. Everything was going to plan. I had arrived!

Paul lived with his boyfriend in Barons Court. Their weekly schedule revolved around a Saturday night party at the seminal dance club, Troll, a Sunday 'come down' in front of the TV, and a week of work and exercise. Harder drugs offered a solution to my pain and I fell naturally into the boys' routine.

I was warmly welcomed into the world of MDMA where everything starts with an E. Where smiley faces beam from every corner, flashing strobes project the scene like a flickering vintage movie, and whistles pierce the deafening soundtrack, urging on the madding crowd. I found it easy to ride the initial head rush when the drugs took their hold, before I lost myself on the dance floor as the music pulsated through my body, drum and bass fusing with my heart and beating a tribal rhythm until sunrise.

The first time I took Ecstasy I was so high I thought I could actually die right there and then – and die the happiest person in the entire world. I was Miss Thing. My name was on the list. I'd found a groove in a record that always ended up on a dance floor or a house party somewhere, always in the company of a sparkly crowd. This *was* ecstasy, and it always left me wanting more. We took LSD to accentuate the high, sometimes watching Walt Disney films on acid before going to the clubs, starting off our evening by crawling out of some Soho cinema on our knees in hysterical laughter.

Paul and his boyfriend usually insisted that I came back and stayed after the club, where I would make up a bed on the sofa and sleep until throat-scorching, brain-aching dehydration propelled me to the refrigerator for orange juice. Once they brought two men back from the club and I lay on the floor, watching TV, still tripping on my LSD while their preliminary foursome got warmed up. I think this awkward moment was when I realized I needed a partner. I threw out a prayer to the Universe for that prince on his white horse to hurry up and rescue me.

Paul C was the answer to that prayer. A few days later he appeared, making his way through the crowd of clubbers around 2 a.m., the time when jittery excitement gave way to the lower key, but no less intense, smacked-out buzz of junkie satisfaction. Steps away from the dance floor, I was sitting by an aquarium filled with tropical fish, chatting with friends, happily taking in the contented scene before me. I smiled over at a happy-looking guy, who beamed back with the most radiant smile I had ever seen. A light seemed to shine from him as he walked over and sat down beside me, announcing as he did, 'I'm coming to talk to you now!' Although this kind of approach was fairly typical rave behaviour, within minutes we were chatting as though we had been reunited after many years apart.

Paul C had a compelling charm, a winning combination of politeness and naivety. His face was almost cherubic, his brown eyes framed with long dark lashes and a perfect smile. I made him laugh and when he did I wanted to kiss him, to hold him tight and never let him go. So I did kiss him. Right there on the floor, with angelfish gliding in the aquarium above our heads, and the dance floor smoke creating a fairy-dust mist beneath us. He held my hand as tightly as I held his and in this moment, the drugs racing through our blood and our hearts beating fast, we melted together. He took me home, not on a white horse, but in his dark-silver sports car, and after more drugs and laughter we slept together.

What I loved most about Paul was his rebelliousness. He came from the debutante world, but was the black sheep of his family, as evidenced by his recent appearance in a *News of the World* double-page spread. His photograph, spliff in one hand and his arm around another toga-wearing party-maker, revelling at some boy band's party, featured under the screaming headline, *POPSTAR'S ECSTASY ORGY,* which his parents saw before he did, choking on their Sunday breakfast as they took in the scene.

Paul and I were never destined for socialite wedlock. Our lifestyle left us worse for wear, and as our relationship progressed, it roller-coasted between intense partying and intense work (me doing a five-day week, him seven, running his own business) while trying to catch up on enough sleep to recover before the next drug binge. One Saturday afternoon Paul's mother invited us to her house for tea with the editor of *Tatler*. We were still spaced out from the night before and I took an instant dislike to the editor's snobbish manner. Paul's mother, who must have caught the way I was scowling at him, took a huge vase of flowers from the mantelpiece and strategically positioned them on the table so that he couldn't see my face.

Paul C's best friend, John, belonged to a wider group my friends called the 'A Gays', a reference to Armistead Maupin's *Tales of the City*. They were all stunning, with interesting careers and often outrageous lifestyles. John was special, with his gentle, humorous, forgiving view of the world and his relentlessly optimistic approach to life, despite having been diagnosed as HIV positive. I loved John and also his long-time companion Jacques, who designed dresses for real princesses, and Adam, John's brother, who was close friends with Kenny, the iconic radio presenter and TV entertainer. Kenny had been diagnosed with HIV too and the media had savaged him.

They all embraced me as the little one of their gang, especially once Paul and I moved into his Fulham flat together. When John and Adam lived in New York for a while, we visited them often, celebrating Kenny's birthday on Christmas Day in Greenwich Village with roast 'E', and I took my first cocaine while chatting with him about wallpaper colours for his London apartment. We went out dancing almost every night. On New Year's Day I bumped into Marc Almond again, in Mars, a dark super-cool club in the meatpacking district, long before the meatpacking district was new and shiny. I spontaneously shouted out to him, 'Marc!' He spun around, looking expectantly in my direction but was confused when he didn't recognise my face. 'It's OK', I shrugged with a smile, 'it doesn't matter.'

This random exchange with my poster boy of a decade earlier came somewhere in the middle of a 48-hour rave that had already gone way beyond any teenage dreams. The same evening I'd noticed Madonna hanging out with her friends in the Roxy before I danced on stage at the Limelight with Leroy from *Fame: The Movie*. That was a 'Ruthie' moment, when I'd felt myself in the spotlight, aware of all the people on the dance floor cheering, only to look to my side and have Gene Anthony Ray beaming back at me. A few hours later, after yellow cab rides that bumped us madly at startling speeds between venues, Grace Jones was forced to climb over John and me as we lay in a giggling heap, pouring out our hearts to each other on the Sound Factory floor.

On our nights in, Paul, John and I would lie on the sofa, gazing up at the Empire State Building perfectly framed in our apartment window. Lit a different colour each evening, we used to guess what shade it would be that night, what time it would be switched off, and whether it faded out or if the lights would snap off all at once. We missed the 'magic moment' so many times before we finally saw those lights blink out. The fun was most definitely in the anticipation.

Sadly, the lows mirrored the highs. Behind closed doors Paul and I bickered and danced around the subject of commitment, both of us bewildered. We were the best of friends and the worst of friends, acting out our frustrations and fear of intimacy with each other. Later that year, on vacation at Fire Island, we hardly spoke for a week then made up on the very last day before the boys joined us from Manhattan. My heart falls heavily when I think back to how much Paul and I hurt each other as we floundered. This was my relationship pattern now, Paul being the third boyfriend with whom I'd acted out a cycle of intense closeness followed by raging hurt; as if the rage could make up for my father, or wash away that schoolteacher. I tried to replay the tape so I could 'fix' it this time. Instead it was a layer of damage upon another layer of damage.

Addiction is mental. It manifests as an insatiable desire to be on the battlefield, the unbearable pain of being wounded there, and the complete powerlessness to vacate the horror. The heartbreaking truth of love addiction is that it happens right where the hope for love exists. Love becomes tangled, confusing, desperate, right there. The very love that you seek, that you give your heart to, is what hurts you the most.

Back in the UK, in the midst of the party, HIV was sweeping through the gay community. With no cure in sight, numerous people were losing their lives to AIDS-related illnesses. There was little public sympathy or understanding. In Troll one evening, again by the aquarium of beautiful fish, I was introduced to Kevin, a director of the Terrence Higgins Trust.

I asked Kevin how I could volunteer to help, and he said I would make a great buddy. The role of a buddy was to provide emotional support and companionship for someone with HIV – who often faced not only a potentially terminal illness but also rejection by family and friends. Could I help someone who was inevitably scared and isolated?

There was a thorough selection process involving a series of interviews followed by a residential training weekend. There I bonded with special people, most notably the chair of the training team, a sensitive man called Jonathan. He inspired and moved me to tears with his personal testimony of companionship on the journey to his friend's death. Shortly afterwards Jonathan introduced me to Paul S, a thirty-four-year-old service user in the grip of several AIDS-related illnesses with little chance of survival.

Paul S was the third significant Paul who hallmarked my life. We first met at the Chelsea and Westminster hospital. It was my job to drive him home, and it was the final part of the selection process. He, as the service user, had the final decision on whether I would get the job. I had been warned that Paul S could be challenging, but an extraordinary and special soul if he trusted you. He was hooked up to a blood machine and I saw him before he saw me. He looked sad but when our eyes met his face lit up. It was love at first sight.

Paul had a number of illnesses and was taking a potent drug called AZT. His most dangerous illness was cryptosporidium, he told me, carried by London pigeons. His immune system couldn't fight it and antibiotics could only keep it under moderate control. It attacked the gut and gave him pain and diarrhoea. You could tell that Paul had once been a shockingly handsome man, tall and athletic with blond curly hair. For many years he'd walked on the wild side, travelling the world as an escort to wealthy companions. He described himself as an orphan, brought up in children's homes or by foster parents who were no longer around. He was an antiques dealer by profession. When he became ill he had broken all ties with his group of friends, hinting at a story he was reluctant to share.

As I helped Paul to steady himself on his feet after his transfusion he called me his 'angel'. When I asked him later what he wanted from our relationship he said,

'A soul mate to go all the way with me – to the very last breath I take.'

'OK. I'll do it', I said, 'but don't expect too much.'

The truth is I had to do it. There was no doubt in my mind.

For the next nine months I saw Paul three times a week. We had some good times and some tough times. He needed way more love and attention than I could possibly give, and it was a constant battle to keep my boundaries in place. We grew incredibly fond of each other, sometimes bickering when he became a shameless passenger-seat driver, and sometimes falling happily asleep during those soporific Saturday afternoon black-and-white movies on TV. While he was still well enough, he would bring me small antique treasures back from the King's Road. When he was sick I would visit him in various hospitals and clinics. We talked for hours about everything under the sun, including his death, whenever it would come. I was his advocate, one hundred percent on his side. I worked with hospital staff, hospice nurses, social workers. I fought his battles when he wasn't strong enough and let him fall asleep in my arms before I left him to face another night alone.

Once he begged me to stay the night with him because he was so frightened. His stomach was hurting way beyond the pain that any drugs could ease, and he was rigid with fear that he wouldn't make it through the night. It was a boundary buddies weren't allowed to cross, but it broke my heart to drive away that night. It was a hot summer evening, heavy traffic angrily growling its way through the Euston underpass at rush hour. I was exhausted. Depleted. I felt so guilty. How I hated rules sometimes. I was desperate for a joint, something to ease my own pain, a way to switch off and not think about the situation any more.

When I arrived home I was surprised to find a beautiful woman sitting on my sofa, sipping a glass of wine and laughing with her friend Sean, who was lodging with Paul C and me for a while. She was introduced as Louise, and as we immersed ourselves in easy conversation, I felt that I was making a friend who understood and accepted me exactly as I was. Louise was a kindred spirit and she felt like a gift from the Universe. When she told me she was leaving in a few weeks time for Los Angeles, to live there, I said, in words hauntingly reminiscent of Paul S, 'We'd better make the most of the time we've got.' A friendship was born that night which not only saved my sanity in those crazy weeks ahead, but has lasted strong and true to this day.

During the final week of his life Paul S told me how much he loved me and how, if he were a well man, he would marry me without a doubt. I pointed out that if he'd been a well man we wouldn't have met in the first place. He said he would wait my entire life and be there for me when my time came. I made him promise never to appear as a ghost given that his ghoulish appearance would probably put me in an early grave too. He promised that he wouldn't. But, after I'd thought about it, I asked if he could sometimes give me a sign that he really was watching over me, especially if I were going through difficult times and needed his reassurance. He considered it for a second and then said, 'Well, I'm very good with electricity.'

Once we shared a brief but intense kiss on his hospice bed, a boundary that was far too close for comfort. But we stopped there. I think Paul found peace in knowing that the last relationship in his life was pure and true, and that he had found love, albeit platonic. Eventually the cryptosporidium took hold. Two nights later he had such violent and uncontrollable diarrhoea that it flooded his bed. Without embarrassment

I helped two nurses mop it up from the floor by the bucket full. I loved him like a brother and a friend and cared little about his shit, his sick, his saliva, his blood – all of which I had come into contact with at some point. In fact I made a point of sharing cups and straws with him. I wanted him to feel normal. There were many things that were messy about our friendship, because we were human beings in extraordinary circumstances, and on reflection everything around us was even messier than that. We did our best and I have no regrets.

I remember the last time we spoke. I'd popped into the Lighthouse hospice to see him. It was Saturday evening – my night out. The atmosphere in his room was great. He was in good spirits despite being bedbound on an inflatable bed to ease the pressure on his skin and bones. We shared a few jokes and sang our 'I love yous' as I breezed out. I had a miserable time in the club that night. I took LSD yet nothing inspired me and the drugs worked in the opposite way. I sat alone by the dance floor, full of dread. Eventually we made it home after a long night. At 7am when the phone rang I'd had an hour's sleep. One of the hospice staff said that I should come straight away. So I showered, ate scrambled eggs and went.

Nothing could have prepared me for the scene I was to face. Paul had gone. In his place was a waxwork that didn't even look like him. His skin had changed colour and texture and he had a contorted expression. I stood there frozen in shock, the LSD now finally kicking in, playing with my vision, exaggerating every detail. A nurse explained that Paul had experienced a mild seizure that morning which left him unable to talk. He had barely regained consciousness, and they said he would probably pass at some point today. This was it. The day Paul had prepared for. He'd heard that dying felt like an orgasm and wondered if it were true. I guess he was going to find out.

We settled down to business: him lying there, breathing,

with his eyes all askew, me holding his hand and wondering what was going to happen next. Then I had the idea that even if he couldn't see or move he might still be able to hear me. And I thought about what I would want to hear right now, to feel reassured. So I started to tell him how everything was OK. That he didn't deserve this. That he hadn't done anything wrong and that nothing bad was going to happen to him. That there was nothing to be scared of, that he was a good person, that I was with him every step of the way, and that I loved him very much.

All of a sudden, the strangest thing happened. First Paul's throat, then his face changed colour as the blood rushed back into it. His eyes came into focus, and he looked straight at me, deep into my eyes. A tear ran slowly down his cheek.

'Oh you can hear me', I said, as I stroked his head. He tried to speak. We smiled into each other's eyes. I reassured him again, that everything was going to be OK. I can't articulate the deep sense of knowing that Paul had resolved something, but I had the strongest feeling that right then he forgave himself. In that moment, everything really was OK.

The energy shifted as Paul vomited. We were both surprised and he panicked. The nurse came back and calmed him down. She offered more medication, something to stop the sickness and something to help him sleep. I asked Paul to squeeze my hand if he wanted it. He thought for a moment then did so, nodding a little as he did. I told him to rest well and to have some great stories for when I saw him again. The nurse put more meds in his syringe driver and shortly afterwards he fell into a deep sleep.

Like so many times before, I sat by his bed, listening to the whirr of the driver against the background hum of hospital activity. But this was for the last time. Two of his friends arrived and we all sat together. By now my eyelids were heavy. Paul's breathing rattled and eventually it slowed right down until it was shallow and quiet. And finally, at around 9pm, with the haunting lyrics of 'Unfinished Sympathy' embracing the room – *Like a soul without a mind, like a body without a heart, I'm missing every part*[3] – Paul's expression changed and his eyes raised to the ceiling. There was a smile on his face as he took his last breath, which didn't look too far away from a gentle orgasm.

It was hard to tell the difference between the Paul who had been breathing and the Paul who wasn't breathing any more. He was still warm, the room still full of his presence. For a while I didn't want to leave. I just wanted to stroke his head and kiss his hands. But eventually it was time. Paul C drove us home. When we got back I headed straight for the bathroom at the top of the house to run a bath. And then, quite remarkably as I made my way up each flight of stairs, crawling with exhaustion now, every single light bulb, one by one, blew as I switched it on. By the time I'd reached the top floor, I was left kneeling in the bathroom in complete darkness. I shook my head and laughed. My heart was alight. Paul had gone nowhere. He was right by my side.

Chapter Three

Animality

Rage is the world of hell, greed is that of hungry spirits,
foolishness is that of animals.
The Object of Devotion for Observing the Mind[1]

A basic life condition with a valuable function. The drive to eat, drink, sleep, fight, procreate… We need these instincts to survive. But if they take over, so does an animalistic state of life where the big intimidate the small and the weak cower before the strong. Dog eat dog. Fight or flight. Life at best, becomes little more than a means of survival.

Paul didn't survive, of course. I did, and with that I faced the inevitable guilt that hit me in the wake of his passing. I was only twenty-three years old as I held the hand of a frightened thirty-five-year-old man. I saw his body ravaged by illness and witnessed a young man turn old and eventually into a corpse right before my eyes. I stared death in the face.

As Paul's registered next of kin I organised death certificates, his funeral and tried to respect his last wishes. I tried to make light of it, denying how I really felt, as if I would be failing somehow if I admitted how upset I was. My friends and work colleagues were supportive, but I couldn't accept their sympathy; instead I reached further into my work with the Terrence Higgins Trust for deeper validation and understanding.

Set against the backdrop of an escalating number of service users and the increased demand for buddies, I decided to become a buddy trainer and share my experience. So, one sunny Friday afternoon I joined the training team as they drove out of town to initiate the next group of volunteers. It was a new beginning. Pulling up on the crunching gravel drive of Bore Place, a charming old manor house set in the softly rolling Kent countryside, my heart lifted. I felt that I had something important to contribute.

The training was designed to brief buddies on their function, provide guidelines and information to support their role, and encourage participation in a peer support network. The workshops began on the Friday evening and finished on Sunday afternoon, after which members of the training team would debrief before making their way back to London ready for our professional jobs on Monday morning. It was challenging, physically exhausting, and utterly compelling.

I had always worked hard to survive. As a child of eight I had persuaded myself that I could protect myself from punishment, particularly from my schoolteacher and my father, if I did well in my studies. Later on, achieving high grades for university secured an exit route from home. I'd also earned money from the age of fourteen, desperate to be independent. The first job was a paper round delivering a huge sack of newspapers to the neighbourhood. This is when I discovered my love of early mornings – the peace and quiet, the early dawn light, even the crisp darkness of winter mornings, and feeling so awake and invigorated before the rest of the world woke up. I was paid £1.75 for a six-day week. The money went straight into a post office account, and when I'd saved enough I bought a brand new Speedo for my diving competitions. At sixteen, I collected glasses in a city-centre bar. During sixth form I worked every weekend as a chambermaid at a local hotel. The work was strenuous, the hours long, but it paid well and it was a scream, racing with my co-worker to see who could make the fastest bed. And now as a young woman, I was similarly driven to working as hard as possible to control my destiny. Hard work never scared me; on the contrary I thrived on it.

I'd first hit London in 1990. The UK was deep in recession with queues of unemployed job-seekers twisting out of the benefits offices. Work was scarce and because of this I fell into one of the few growth industries of the early '90s: IT services. Even though I had never used a computer before, within three weeks I'd learned enough to teach City boys their spreadsheets and secretaries their word processors. The PC revolution had begun, and I had serendipitously become a facilitator. Teaching software skills to the banks and corporates opened up a new world. Suddenly I found myself on the inside of London's shiny new glass buildings with a purpose and soon realized that I could earn far more in sales than in a classroom delivering training. So I switched companies to work for a man called Ken, who took me under his wing and I hooked myself into becoming his new rising star. It was the perfect place for my workaholic tendencies to take root.

My job was to cultivate client relationships so that they would keep their business with us. I had an expense account and a company car, and my clients were nice people. I made two important relationships during this time that marked my success, one with a startlingly bright woman called Cathy who ran the training programme at London Underground; another with Peaches at the BBC World Service. Cathy represented diligence and together we made a mark in our respective workplaces. In Peaches I made a close friend who shared my love of dancing and taking drugs. We would often conduct business on the steps of Covent Garden plaza whilst smoking a joint, and sometimes we'd lose ourselves on the Ministry of Sound dance floor until sunrise. Success was relatively easy. It was a buoyant market and we had a good time. We lunched at cool restaurants like Langhams alongside Michael Caine. I also ran the Eurotunnel account and got to shuttle between Biggin Hill and Calais in a twin-engined plane.

That was all easy, and lucrative, but it was my voluntary work that provided a greater sense of purpose. I felt at home with the other volunteers, and part of something important. We met weekly to review and develop course material and we received training of our own, sometimes at weekends, sometimes in the evenings. One month I calculated I had put in one hundred hours of Terrence Higgins Trust work on top of my paid full-time job. Hiding behind a heartfelt desire to change the world for the better, all of my addictions were at play. Workaholic perfectionism was the bass line. If I were good enough I would be liked. If I were good enough I would be loved. If I were good enough...

My sex and love addiction played somewhere in the middle, discordant and unpredictable and dangerously seductive. I was as needy as I was autonomous, and these conflicting mindsets created an internal battle that made it impossible either to feel satisfied with Paul C or to leave him. The melody was sung through my friendships which, although genuine, were shot through with drinking and drugs, highs and lows.

My blissed-out nights with Peaches could plummet to earth in a moment. One evening we took one Ecstasy pill after the next, convinced they didn't work, only for them to hit home all at once and send us into orbit. What seemed like days later we lay on a sofa at a stranger's house, the DJ from the club now playing in the living room, as we declared our undying love and friendship. That same weekend ended with me hurling my cannabis pipe out of the window of a taxi in desperation as we sped away from a hip-hop gig gone wrong.

I met a genuine guy called Malcolm whilst dancing on the same podium at Heaven. We met up again the next day in a Sunday-afternoon club in a basement restaurant in Holborn and were best friends by the end of the weekend. But eventually our common ground was extinguished when we were too exhausted to strut around a dance floor any longer. Similarly I shared a deep connection with a precious man in the training team called Sean. We leaned on each other emotionally, so heavily in fact, that eventually we fell over. It was unsustainable.

Yet, friendships were my lifeline. I was no less honest with my friends than I was with myself, and in this respect I was genuine. People like Michael, my co-chair of the buddy training team, also driven by his desire to challenge injustice, became my brother in arms.

This was 1992. Pre-email and pre-mobile phone. A time mostly lost, either from death or burnout, yet I remember these unique training weekends like they were yesterday. Sunday was the emotional climax. Everyone explored their mortality and thought about their own funeral. Sometimes I shared my experience of Paul's life and death. Then we talked about suicide. What if our service user wanted to take their life? How could we support them without becoming an accomplice? How did this conflict with our personal views? We faced questions about euthanasia head-on in extraordinary circumstances. And through it all we pondered the effect that war must have had on our grandparents, when they had lost so many young men of their generation. How different were the heroes of their generation compared with ours?

We finished the weekend with an exercise called the Love Tunnel. Each person would walk across the room with their eyes closed, their fellow participants touching them lightly as they moved through. Sometimes I would recoil, unable to receive acknowledgement and support from my fellows as I passed between their hands. Afraid of letting down my guard, I hid behind a wall of cynicism rather than admitting the trauma that this exercise provoked in me.

Once a journalist infiltrated the course, posing as a trainee. After dinner on Saturday everyone relaxed and had a few drinks to unwind together. That particular evening I felt proud to be part of a group of such courageous individuals, people not only volunteering their time, but also taking on a challenging role in the AIDS movement. Shortly afterwards one of the shitty tabloids ran a piece under the headline *SEX AND DRUGS ON AIDS TRAINING WEEKEND*. To my knowledge there were never any drugs taken, and let's face it, I would probably have known. It hurt the buddy service and raised questions that we had to answer. For all the times we stood there professionally, dedicated to providing the best, just one relaxed evening and our opponents, sly, disguised and voiced by a homophobic rag, took advantage.

Working as a buddy made me think about other people: the people who weren't on the dance floor tonight, who weren't at the chill-out party this morning, who wouldn't be at Gay Pride this year. It helped me stay in touch with reality and take personal responsibility for what was going on. Training buddies put a unique lens on the struggle for survival. We may have been powerless over HIV and its impact, but we found a way to support someone at the heart of their struggle. Different people had different ways. This was ours.

My greatest regret during this time was the break down of my relationship with Paul C. While I was away on the training weekends, he carried on as before, and I would come home to find the remains of another wild party night in our home, an array of ashtrays and bottles for me to clear up, with a wide-eyed Paul tired, hung over and rarely pleased to see me. We were growing further apart, a gulf widening between us that we could not bridge. For a while we lived almost separate lives in the same house, sharing a familiar and unspoken friendship at best.

I flew to Los Angeles to see Louise and gather my thoughts. Since Louise had moved to LA we had written to each other constantly, our airmail letters winging back and forth across the Atlantic. Now that Louise was settled into a job and had a place in West Hollywood, I took my first trip to California with excitement, so happy to be reunited with my closest friend. Our mutual friend Robert also joined us. I fell in love with California, the laid back, super-cool LA lifestyle and of course its big blue ocean. We took a road trip to San Francisco like Thelma and Louise complete with our very own Brad Pitt in the back seat. This was my first drive, now for real, along the Big Sur on Highway 1, and my heart released. We walked for hours along the white sands of Malibu and Carmel, breathing in the salty air, feeling the wind in our hair and the sun on our faces, watching whales blowing water as they rose above the waves and plunged down again.

One day I sat on Venice Beach alone, struggling with my thoughts, struggling to know how to face life without Paul, knowing in my heart that it was inevitable. A Rasta man quietly appeared by my side and offered me his joint as he sat down next to me. He didn't want anything, just to talk, and without me sharing anything, he offered up some words of encouragement, saying that I was a strong woman and that I was going to be OK. As quickly as he had appeared, he vanished and I went back to find the others, feeling strangely empowered.

I phoned Paul sometime later. He told me that he had taken a woman back to our house and slept with her. Nauseous, jealous, desperate disappointment sank to the pit of my stomach. There it was again, that sickening feeling of love's betrayal. I trembled with anger and fear. Then I defiantly hardened my heart just a little bit more, breathing smoke deeply into my lungs, letting the drugs fog out my feelings in a thick cloud of denial.

Back in the UK it was time to face more endings. John was sick. His HIV had developed into pneumonia and he came back to live with Jacques, his long-time companion with whom he'd shared a home before he'd left for New York. They lived around the corner from us in Islington, and I would often go there with Paul, who visited most days. I adored Jacques and could see why John had chosen to spend his last months in his compassionate and tireless presence. Jacques oozed class and grace, never once complaining about the task in hand. His home radiated indulgence and love, wrapping John in protected warmth. Another friend of Paul and John's from school, a brilliant doctor called Imogen, was on constant call. I felt drawn to support her like a sister, as she bravely became a rock for everyone. She was everything that I had failed to be for Paul, for John, for myself. Yet this was my family, and I couldn't bear to leave.

John deteriorated rapidly, forced to rely on everyone to nurse him, which he found difficult. He asked his father, an eminent psychiatrist, to give him an overdose to hasten things before they reached their inevitable conclusion. When John awoke from what should have been a fatal prescription, I sat with him. He told me that after the overdose, when he had woken up, he'd spent a few moments wondering where he was, hoping with all his heart that he was in heaven. When he realized he was conscious and still alive, he knew he was in hell. Before becoming ill, John had been the strongest, most optimistic person anyone could have met, but illness and death scared him. He found his last few months humiliating. I could see it in his eyes.

That was the last conversation I had with John. Because of his loyalty to Paul he stopped acknowledging me in those final weeks. As much as I understood, it hurt. Then one morning Paul said, 'I think you should move out.' I didn't resist, as much as I felt my insides crumble. He was right. It had gone on for long enough. I put on a brave face and left our beautiful home for a small apartment that was only yards away. It was worlds apart.

There was little I liked about my new home. It was on the top floor of a building that housed a crack den in the basement, and it stank of the previous residents. I spent my first night shivering in fear. I scrubbed and painted the apartment, but it was inside my head that the real clean-up was needed. Fear seemed to run through everything I thought, everything I said and everything I did. I was scared of not succeeding in my career. I was scared of being alone. I was scared of being unloved. I was scared of not being 'someone'. Everything was driven by fear.

A few weeks later Imogen called to say that John had passed away. I went to the house after everyone had left and spent some time with John's peaceful body, glad to see that the strains of his illness, which had aged him so rapidly, had now given way to a smooth complexion of restfulness. He looked young again, his skin translucent and light. I stroked his head. I said I was sorry, and Imogen told me that John did truly care for me. At his funeral I only just held it together while screaming inside. It was the last time I saw Kenny, who was also getting ill. He passed away some time afterwards. Today he embraced me as warmly as ever, wanting to know what had happened with Paul and me. I couldn't even speak. Afterwards a few of us numbed out on another narcotic cocktail, but nothing could make this feel better. John had gone. Paul and I were over. What was the point?

Of all drugs, I loathe cocaine. I have witnessed the most intelligent, sensitive and loving people transform into monsters from the minute the phone call to the dealer is made. Some of my most selfish, self-centered or self-destructive behaviour has been under the influence of this substance. Cocaine releases adrenaline which speeds up the heart rate and prepares the body for fight or flight, creating a panic-stricken environment which people project into a bullying and aggressive state of mind, needing to be 'one up' on everyone else around them. And oh, how it dumbs down any real emotions, disconnecting the user from their true feelings.

If you consider what cocaine is made of and the journey

it has taken, it's easy to see why. Soaking the leaves of a coca plant in petroleum or kerosene produces the base product. After this the leaves are transported to another factory. People are often killed along the way. When the drug finally arrives on the streets to be sold, more people are killed. Cocaine has blood all over it. Some reaches the West by boat, some is delivered by mules. A mule is often a teenage girl, lured by the money or the chance to leave her country. She swallows up to sixty ounces of the drug, still wrapped in plastic. If the plastic bursts while the wraps are inside her stomach, she dies and dealers cut the drugs out of her dead body before it is dumped. If you use cocaine, you could be inhaling the inside of a dead girl's stomach.

After John's passing I was caught out there. Away from the security of living with Paul, I embraced this drug of paradox with its capacity to heighten the animal instinct to survive – aiding stamina and performance on one hand, yet fostering delusion, bad judgment and self-destruction on the other. I pushed myself ever harder through my daily schedule at work, seeking bigger promotions in order to increase my salary. I sedated myself into sleep at night with Valium or Triazepam. Up, then down, but always disconnected.

Then came a crash, quite literally, as I sped through familiar streets, nearly home at the end of a very long week. I shot a red light fast and collided with another car doing the same. My car spun, lights around me moving in endless slow motion before it came to a standstill. My heart sank. This was bad. I jumped out of my car and ran towards the other car. To my relief the driver, a woman, was already running towards me. We stood on the pavement, facing each other,

'Are you OK?'

'Yes, are you?'

'Yes.' We spontaneously hugged each other in relief, and exchanged a knowing look.

'We don't need the police.'

'No.'
'I'm so glad you are OK.'
'Yes, me too.'
The car was a write-off. I shook to the bones all night. Sooner or later surviving on animal instincts becomes a poor and lonely substitute for life.

It was a wake-up call of sorts. I knew I had to slow down, take some breaths, be more careful, stop putting so much pressure on myself. But how? I knew I wanted to find peace, but I had no idea where to find it. I pulled back on the cocaine, yet searched once again for a relationship fix. In the light of three failed relationships with men, I concluded I must be gay, reflecting on the brief affair with my friend at university and recent flirtations with other gay women around me. When I was introduced to a glamorous American TV journalist, sassy and confident, we spent a night together, during which I felt so deeply connected with this aspect of my sexuality that I got caught up in the fantasy of moving to New York and being with her. And then came a call from Louise, who was getting married in Las Vegas. Would I be her maid of honour? My American friend suggested I visit her en route, so I made the flight bookings and prepared for a whirlwind trip – ten thousand miles and three US cities in five days. Maybe it wasn't time to slow down after all…

I set off at lunchtime from Heathrow, my head already in the clouds. The weekend was a blast, spending one night in Los Angeles for the wedding rehearsal, before flying to Las Vegas where we stayed at the Pyramid hotel with its view across the desert. My cocktail of choice was Triazepam with champagne, and by the time of the wedding, I was comfortably wrapped up in a soft and fuzzy glow, bathing in the presence of the beautiful group of people around me and enchanted with the buzz of the place. We arrived at the wedding chapel without the required marriage license, so we all piled into a car and made our way down the Strip to a government building. Queuing up along with all the other couples was one of those rare moments where the natural boundaries of class, age and wealth were completely irrelevant. My eyes widened as I took in the sight before me. A priceless collection of Las Vegas wedding parties sparkled, all in one room together – all ethnicities, all shapes and sizes, a mish-mash of bridal styles, and a variety of costumes, some of them quite possibly from the fancy dress shop next door...

By the time we arrived back at the chapel for the service I was in high spirits. Louise's best male friend, Graham, was a witness and the two of us stood by her for the ceremony. Already giddy, everything somehow became highly amusing and when it came to Louise stating her vows, we had a fit of the giggles. I have always struggled with the giggles, sometimes taking chunks out of my mouth in an effort to bite back the laughter. This was one of those occasions. I tried the best I could, but by the time the ceremony was over so was any future relationship I was ever going to have with Louise's freshly married husband. He switched from Jekyll to Hyde in the moment following the bridal kiss, and my blood ran cold with the icy stares that he shot in my direction, reserving his displeasure exclusively for me. I sank into a trough of shame that should have been reserved solely for the turquoise nylon boob-tube wedding dress that I had witnessed in the registrar office a few hours earlier. I made my excuses, assuring Louise that I was fine and just needed to rest, and I retreated to the hotel room where I spent the rest of the night alone before catching my flight to New York in the morning.

New York welcomed me like it always had with its characterful inhabitants and its electric atmosphere. And the time with my friend was both precious and futile, a fresh manifestation of my sex and love addiction, an indulgent physically charged high, underpinned with a deep, heart-felt emotional binding of two souls in a desperate longing. I tore myself away, comforted only by the promise of her trip to London in a month's time.

Back in London I moved house to share a place with a friend called Kit, deep in the heart of the West End. The peace that I yearned for was more elusive than ever as I now slept in a room close to Shaftesbury Avenue with its thousands of black cabs turning their engines morning, noon and night while drunken revelers cruised the streets until dawn. It was good to be in Kit's company though, the warden of an old people's sheltered dwelling, and a lifeline to me too in those turbulent days. Moreover, there was an outside municipal swimming pool set in the grounds behind us, and I would swim there every morning before work, sucking in the fresh morning air within the pulsating soundscape of West End life. I spent Christmas with Kit, pining for my American friend, counting the days until she would arrive, only to be let down at the eleventh hour. She called to say she was back in the arms of her long-term girlfriend and wouldn't be able to see me. I felt my stomach sink in its now familiar way, another wave of dreadfulness, adding to the feeling of being just a little bit more useless than I was before.

There was a friend of Paul S called Natasha, whom he had introduced a few days before he passed away. A post-operative trans-sexual, shockingly beautiful, incredibly flamboyant, a model and performer – she stood out wherever she went. I was drawn to Natasha in many ways. Emotionally we were strongly connected. She was there the day Paul died, and our shared experience had created a strong bond between us. But it was a deeper issue that pulled me towards her.

Self-image had been a struggle from as long as I could remember. I had been physically awkward to the point of self-loathing long before puberty had hit. When it did, sex had been the fix, a way of getting out of my body, which felt so excruciatingly uncomfortable to be in. By my twenties, however, sexuality was compounding the discomfort. I was attractive for sure, not necessarily in a conventional sense, but I ticked all the boxes and was often described in flattering terms. Yet there was a huge disparity between what I saw in the mirror and how I actually felt. Starving myself at university had been a symptom of this body dysmorphia. Extreme workouts at the gym were all part of it too. But a physical disconnectedness was now escalating to the point that I was even starting to question my gender. *What was being a woman actually supposed to feel like?* I really didn't know.

Natasha became my smoking partner and I would visit her place almost daily after work on my way home, my first chance to unwind. Our conversations were open and honest, and we benefited from each other's contrasting yet unexpectedly aligned perspectives. And did Natasha know how to have fun…! After a day in the office I was happy to sit back and let someone else take control, and Natasha was easy to follow. We would go out often, swishing between the Soho bars and clubs, any night of the week. Natasha not only knew the scene, she *was* the scene and when she arrived at a club door staff would either jump to attention or disappear into the club straight away, returning shortly afterwards with the promoter or manager who would welcome us in.

I think I idolized and feared Natasha in equal measure and I was swept along on her dramatic coat-tails far more than was good for me. Once she talked me into creating a drag show with her, which we rehearsed for weeks before performing it at several drag bars, including the top bar at Heaven. It was a grotesque show, twenty minutes of peculiar outrageousness that had us dressed in various outfits from Underground workers to YMCA dancers, with Natasha impersonating Barry Manilow doing 'Lola the Showgirl' and me playing a transvestite Little Mermaid singing 'Part of Your World' as I faked a nervous breakdown. We filled condoms with jelly, which we wore inside jock straps, and stuck on facial hair. I looked enough like a man to pass for a young Sean Penn. For the final number we blacked up as '70s soul singers complete with Afro wigs and platform heels. It was surreal and ridiculous, and had audiences stop in their tracks. As much as I enjoyed the attention, when it came to looking good it was Natasha who took the crown, using me as her foil. If there was one person I could not say No to, it was Natasha. But she had a heart of gold.

As soon as she heard that my American friend had left me high and dry, Natasha came flying over, LSD in hand, and announced we were going on a 'helicopter' ride to the bars in my neighbourhood. Glad of a distraction from my freshest heart wound, I willingly agreed. We set off to a place around the corner. The very busy WOW bar was for women only, a scene I was not familiar with since so many of my friends were men. A different kind of buzz stirred the air, and I quickly relaxed into things. After a while Natasha saw someone she knew and brought her over to meet me,

'Ruth! This is Gina. Gina meet Ruth.'

Gina was beautiful and shy. That made me shy too, and we spent some time in an intriguing silence, letting the high-pitched excitement of the women around us drown out our awkwardness. I could tell that Gina was special. She was graceful and gentle, and I loved her energy, the way she just stood by my side, not asking anything of me, but making it clear that she wasn't going anywhere else. I found her presence reassuring. It seemed ages before the night finally ran its course and we were able to negotiate our departure from the bar, dropping off friends on the way before her finally driving us back to my place together. I felt peaceful with Gina. She was calm, and it made me calm too. She did funny things, like play snap with my business cards, and we smoked until dawn, sharing our life stories and our struggles with parents and families. It was Sunday evening before Gina left, almost twenty-four hours after we had met, and it marked the birth of a lifetime's friendship.

As I stood on the balcony that night, watching Covent Garden life play out on the street below, I reflected on what it was to be a woman. Gender, sexuality, womanhood… it all felt so disconnected. The thought of creating and nurturing another human life? It was all I could do to sustain my own. Yet in a moment of hopeful expectation I realized that I had survived – and for the time being at least, that was enough.

Chapter 4

Anger

Anger. Rage. Destruction. The kind of white-hot, fever pitch fury that makes you want to smash an aeroplane into a skyscraper and kill as many people as possible. If there was ever a visual metaphor for anger, Ground Zero is it. The Treasure Tower described in the *Lotus Sutra* was a sparkling, bejewelled monument reaching miles into the sky, representing the vast potential and preciousness of every single human life. Ground Zero was an obliteration, a flattened grave of mangled steel and mass destruction. At the dawn of the twenty-first century, this was our world, a Hollywood horror fantasy that smashed through the borders of reality and blew apart our collective consciousness.

9/11 and the events that followed show how far human beings will go to make their point. How much havoc they are prepared to wreak for the sake of an argument. The result is nothing but pain and loss. And the worst thing? Knowing deep down that it won't resolve anything. All it will prove is that they were this angry – furious and deluded to the extreme. How many people woke up on the morning of 12 September 2001 with a feeling of dread in the pit of their stomach, knowing that things were never going to be the same again? It was a collective heart-sinking moment in time, of which there have already been far too many.

There is a similar heart-sinking, stomach-twisting moment when two people fall out and things go one step too far. A disagreement that becomes abusive and ends up with a physical punch or a vicious verbal blow below the belt. That moment in a bar for example, when a pint of beer gets smashed into someone's face, or when something is said to crush the recipient or incite them to retaliate. The point when someone storms off at a crucial moment in an argument, leaving their companion to settle the restaurant bill and make their way home alone. The point of no return. For no matter what is said or done afterwards, there will always be a scar.

It's not to say that things can't move forward and that positive change can't take place. But that healing takes deep forgiveness on both sides. A mutual desire has to exist, a joint preparedness to dig beneath the argument, beneath the conflict, and find a place of deeper connection. That takes courage, honesty and a willingness to admit to being wrong. Unfortunately people often move away from difference, choosing to stay in the comfort of their own understanding, settling into the conviction that they are right and that it's all the other person's fault. In a Buddhist context this is the world of anger.

There is a line that connects the catastrophic events of 9/11 with the discrete conflicts between two individuals. This line, I believe, is the line of inflated ego, a line that separates people rather than unites them. The line where individuality morphs into individualism. Whenever I cast aspersions on the person that I consider too different for me to understand, I am treading this same line that progresses, eventually, to the justification for mass destruction on a global scale. Whenever

I refuse to see another person's point of view, or when I fight back when someone upsets me, I walk the very same line that does not resolve conflict, but that perpetuates it. Whenever a government, military power or political leader chooses combat over peace talks, they are, in my opinion, doing the same.

By the time I met Gina, six years before the events of 9/11, I was already lost in a very angry world. From a place of crushed self-worth, I inflated my ego to justify my resentment. I was right, the world was wrong. Yet it was fear and shame that drove my self-righteousness, so in this respect, I was wrong and the world was right. My ego yo-yoed between two extremes, both equally judgmental and harsh, both serving to separate and disconnect. I felt that I didn't belong, that I was never good enough. My external Treasure Tower was already an internal Ground Zero, so what was the point?

At the start Gina and I were inseparable. We were the best of friends, with the passion of lovers, drawn to each other with an intense longing. My room was our cocoon, a pleasure dome for lounging, sharing laughs with Kit, sleeping and smoking before we ventured outside for food or clothes. We were both pretty, and made a striking couple, always turning heads as we strolled down Long Acre or across the Piazza.

Yet with our love came pain. Both of us were scarred from our formative experiences. When we locked horns, we exploded. Our arguments often culminated in Gina storming off with me shouting 'I hate you', from my balcony as she disappeared into the crowds of super-hip shoppers. Beneath her gentle demeanour Gina held her own anger, but she was far more moderate than me. Drug use was pushing me into gross avoidance and extreme mood swings. My depression became progressively darker. One night I told Gina I felt that I was standing on a high cliff and something was trying to pull me over the edge. She suggested I get counselling.

Trusting Gina enough to get honest about my internal

struggle was a first step into the years of recovery that followed, but only the first step of thousands. I had a long way to go. I found a counsellor and for our first few sessions I insisted on a pseudonym, such was my paranoia. Things reached a climax the night of the work Christmas party. Early in the evening I was picked out of the crowd by the entertainers who draped a twelve-foot python around my neck. On the photographs I look happy and relaxed. Later, I jumped from a balcony onto the dance floor, stupidly thinking that everyone would catch me. I was so high I hardly noticed the impact of the fall. When Gina collected me, I had lost my voice, was bleeding from my Wonder Woman stunt and I could do nothing but crawl into bed and pass out. Two days later I wanted to die. I knew that I had to stop drinking and taking drugs. One way or another it was going to kill me. I announced my plan to my therapist. Gina breathed an audible sigh of relief, and a few days before Christmas I drew a line in the sand and took a personal vow of sobriety.

It was 1995 and the HIV situation was getting worse, not better. After Paul died in '92 I had buddied a twenty-four-year-old named Alberto for a few weeks before the virus took his life. A third buddy relationship was with William, an early-retired medical doctor who hardly ever needed me. His partner, Andrew, and his sister had persuaded him to take a buddy and he remained unconvinced until the one occasion when he called on my company. Sometimes a buddy relationship was just for that one moment. In William's case I filled an unforeseen gap one evening in the otherwise solid and consistent emotional support from his loved ones. William sadly died at only forty years old, leaving both Andrew and his sister painfully bereaved.

Andrew, an early-retired dentist, asked me to carry on as his buddy. I liked him a lot and I would have been his friend regardless, but he insisted that I took an official role. He didn't want anyone else to be his buddy. He wanted me. Andrew was a lovely man who was incredibly good fun to be with – witty, intelligent, kind and still relatively well. Before I met Gina we would go out to nightclubs and he even helped me decorate my apartment.

Andrew's life was difficult after William died. They had been together for many years, closer than most married couples. Alongside his grief Andrew faced death if medical advances did not move fast enough. In the end, I think I came to rely too much on Andrew's strength and courage. His company was a sanctuary. We broke buddy rules on many occasions, kicking back with a joint and his favourite tea, a pot of Lapsang Souchong and Earl Grey mix. One night we took an acid trip and went to see Jim Carrey's *The Mask*. It stands as one of my favourite drug experiences. I justified this transgression – just as I did everything. The world was against people like me and Andrew; we were perfectly entitled to bend the rules. We talked for hours that night, after the cinema. Our manifesto for life. What was fair and what was not.

When Andrew started to get sick his quality of life declined fast. Depression took hold and I found it hard to give him the support he needed. Nothing could make things better. How could it? How can you help someone feel good about their life when they are suffering so much, emotionally raw from losing the love of their life, don't want to live alone, and know that their own death is just around the corner? My own emotional health was also wearing thin. I managed to stop smoking, sharing a last joint with Andrew on his birthday and vowed that in a year's time I would be celebrating not only him being a year older, but a year of not smoking too. That day did eventually come – but not before Andrew told me that he planned to take his own life.

I had hoped that the elusive cure for HIV would have emerged by now. Andrew's argument, that he couldn't face living on his own, racked me. Was I failing him as a friend by not moving in to care for him? Was I to blame? Thinking back to the buddy guidelines I tried to put my feelings to one side for Andrew's sake. I didn't want things to end this way, so abruptly, with Andrew so angry about the way life had gone for him. But what could I do? What could I change? There was nothing. And as Andrew shared his plan with me – so well thought out, so well prepared – I saw empowerment in his eyes. I saw strength. Life had been out of his control for so long, but finally he could determine the way it would end.

Still living at home, Andrew had saved and stockpiled doses of his prescription morphine. With his medical knowledge, he had devised a way to administer a lethal dose over twenty-four hours. He was 100 percent sure there was double the dosage necessary. And he chose a weekend when his community nurse would visit less frequently, which would give time for the drugs to work. I asked if he was sure.

'Yes', he said. I asked him when.

'This weekend.' Easter.

We had this conversation on the Thursday. He said he wanted to see me the following day so that we could say our goodbyes. He wasn't asking me to help, but he wanted me to 'visit' him on the Sunday morning and find him passed away. It wouldn't be just me. Two more friends would be there. I was sworn to secrecy. It was a buddy's biggest guideline and one that I wanted to honour more than anything.

We said our goodbyes on Good Friday, over our usual pot of tea while Andrew smoked a joint. We ate hot cross buns. He asked me to tell his story one day, in support of euthanasia, which he advocated poignantly and committedly, with his life, and with his death. He fervently hoped that during my lifetime euthanasia would become legal so that people didn't have to suffer the degrading and unbearable existence of being alone in the throes of a terminal illness. He congratulated us on being pioneers. I hugged him, feeling inside that I didn't want to let him go. Andrew wouldn't let us get emotional. I held it in, for his sake. He deserved that. I could do that.

I drove away with tears in my eyes. Despite my peer group work, for all my preaching that confiding in our support groups was the only way to face difficult situations I was isolated in my suffering. I loved Andrew and was as frustrated as he was. We were mirrors to each other, confused and frightened. I kept the secret, scared of what might happen if I didn't. For two nights my sleep was restless and full of lurid dreams. At no point over the weekend did I feel peace, until the Sunday when I woke with an overwhelming sense of calmness that all was well. Maybe Andrew was reunited with William and there was an end to his suffering.

Driving back to Andrew's on that bright Sunday morning I was nervous of what I would find, but prepared, relieved in a way that it would all be over. When I got there, however, it was not the scene I expected. Andrew's nurse opened the door. She said that Andrew was awake but that things were not right. Andrew's other friends arrived. We looked at each other, reading each other's anxiety and concern. Andrew had carried out his plan for sure, taking at least fifteen grams of morphine intravenously, but for whatever reason, he had survived it.

The nurse left us, Andrew in a dozy stupour, on the brink it seemed of life and death. I remembered John's experience of hell. Andrew's was the same. I realized then that euthanasia was like abortion. Abortion is for unwanted life. Euthanasia is for unwanted death. People would do it anyway, simply because they felt they had no choice. And, like backstreet abortions, back street euthanasia also created problems, and it didn't always work. At least if it were lawful, professional medics could administer the process.

At times that day Andrew's breathing became so shallow it reminded me of Paul's last day at the Lighthouse. We were confused. What would Andrew want us to do? We wanted to support him. Eventually we decided that if he were conscious he would want more morphine. We sat around his bed, our hearts in our mouths as we watched the friend who was a nurse put the last remaining dose through the syringe driver. A few hours later Andrew woke up and asked me to roll him a joint. He was devastated. Waking up made things worse not better. He was more depressed, more ill and more lonely than ever. Yes, we celebrated his birthday, and yes I went a whole year without smoking, but it really was no party.

By now I had moved out of the West End to share a flat with Gina. But things had not gone to plan there either. Neither of us was able to commit fully, which prompted a cyclical and frustrating argument. One evening I went out with a friend Gina disliked, and came home to find that she had removed all of her things from our place. I saw red and felt perfectly justified in tearing around to her mother's house in the middle of the night, my stomach churning in panic stricken terror and self-righteous fury. *How could she!*

I woke up the house, Gina, her mother, and a friend of hers whom I strongly disliked, who stood defiantly between Gina and me. I lashed out, and the friend pinned me to the floor, right there on the landing, outside Gina's mother's bedroom. Not only was it one of the least classy moments of my life, it was also a step too far. Gina and I retreated in a furious Mexican standoff, both too indignant to utter another word.

How things could fall apart. Gina was out of my life, and Andrew was soon to follow. He left London to be with his family, far away on the Isle of Man. I'll never forget the feeling as I drove him to the airport for his bleak departure. He was anxious. So was I. A few weeks later, I flew to see him. It was hard to know what to say. Over the course of a cold and wet weekend, I perceived the shadow of a man waiting to die, in pain and powerless over his destiny. He didn't want to leave his room, not even for tea on the seafront. It was a million miles away from the days when we would settle down on the sofa for the evening with good music and an endless stream of lively conversation. As I flew back, shrouded in despair, I felt that the system I had worked for so tirelessly had failed. I had failed. I didn't hear from Andrew again. He passed away peacefully four months later. He was thirty-five. My volunteering days were over. I was as burned out as Andrew's ashes.

The months that followed began to bring some respite and healing for the first time in my life. Regular therapy, the same time each week for two years, created stability and calm. Keeping a clear head by staying off drugs and alcohol was also invaluable. I found self-esteem, and with it gained a more balanced view of myself, a right-sized view, rather than that ego-driven view of 'better or worse than'. I stopped trying to be something I wasn't. Even Gina and I reunited for a while, sharing a few peaceful and supportive months together.

Ken, who had been my boss all along, offered me a position and shares in his new business, an Internet start-up, and at the same time I bought a property in West London. After all those months of work, breathing in, breathing out, facing some demons, the universe responded with abundance. And in the spring following Andrew's death, we held a beautiful memorial for him, remembering the best of times, the Andrew who had lived so vibrantly. Only months later, combination therapy came through the drug trials and into the hands of HIV carriers, some of whom are friends and still living normal lives to this day. Thankfully these AIDS-rife years are now almost forgotten in the UK. But my memories of these brave men and women whose lives touched mine will always live on.

The new job meant long hours and a low salary, but I always knew that the rewards would come. My workaholic tail was up and I threw myself into my career with renewed vigour. It was fun being part of a new project and I was more motivated and clearer than I'd ever been. I wobbled when Gina and I finally separated, pulled apart not by conflict this time but because of the difference in our personal directions. Despite loving her deeply, I never saw us growing old together. Once we were apart, however, I missed her with a desperate longing that nothing could satisfy. It was unbearable. Losing this relationship opened a wound that was so breathtakingly painful that I compulsively reached for the only medicine I knew would soothe it – the club scene and its inevitable cocktail of drugs and sex.

It was fun for a while, but when I heard that Gina had a new girlfriend I crumbled. I fell into a relationship with a woman I found physically unattractive. I exploited her obsession with me, using the cocaine that she sold to minor TV celebrities to distance myself from revolting feelings, my head spinning now with thoughts as deluded as the dirty cloud of powder that I sucked into my lungs. I invited this woman to live with me, and then expected her to cook and clean, making her sleep in a separate room. When we had sex I felt degraded. It took a year to extract myself from this shameful affair, and when I did, I was back at square one. On the surface, to the people I worked with, to the people who knew me, things looked relatively OK. The business was growing fast, I was successful at what I did, and I kept a grip on my health and fitness. But addiction had taken hold, inflating my ego one minute, and crashing it to the floor the next. I slammed down the emotional shutters tighter than ever.

By May 1999 the Internet boom was at its height. After two years of ten-hour days working in a pressurised sales office, we were sold to an American company and I was paid hundreds of thousands of pounds. My stock was worth a million and my regular salary was in six figures. It should have been a fairy-tale ending, the fantasy of my childhood finally coming true. Yet my mental health was in tatters.

I set out to take a break not only from work but also from the addicted lifestyle that had crept up on me again. I learned how to scuba dive at a local facility and then booked a holiday to Thailand for two weeks to complete the course in open water.

At the last minute I impulsively invited a friend of Peaches to go with me, hardly knowing her, but encouraged by the time we had shared over the course of a drug-fuelled weekend in Madrid.

It didn't go well. I found myself seething for most of the time we were away. Her spoilt and petulant attitude was just another reflection of myself, of course, a manifestation of my own neurosis. We bickered constantly about what to do and where to go, each pulling indignantly against the other's ideas. She persuaded me to smoke drugs on the beach one night against my better judgment. I passed out from the strength of the hit. My friend, now petrified, started screaming and trying to shake me awake as I kept slipping back under a dark blanket of unconsciousness, where, to be honest, I felt quite happy to go.

I drew a brief line of sobriety after that episode and found my connection once more beneath the waves, with a scuba license that let me dive deep. Here was my perfect world. Here was peace. Nothing but the sound of my air, breathing in, breathing out, and the sublime physical weightlessness that took all of the pressures of earth from my shoulders. As I floated through magical kingdoms of shimmering turquoise, awestruck by the luminescent fish that bubbled around me, I felt the wonder of life, I felt connected to my source. I would drain my tank to the very last breath before making my way up to the surface, temporarily filled with fresh hope that there was a place for me up there. How could my friend have known what I was going through? After all, I hardly knew myself.

Two weeks away and I came back glowing and clear – and headed straight back into London life and narcotics. Despite our success, work was no less pressured, if anything the stakes seemed to have risen after the buy-out. I was overtired and fed up with my commute to Silicon Ditch every morning.

So I took another trip, this time to India, again with the intention to retreat and get clean. Beachside at Arambol in Goa on the first night I sobbed myself to sleep with loneliness, a razor blade sitting ominously by the bed, as if placed there to taunt me: *You should just end your worthless life.* The next day I met Maria, a stunning girl from the South Pacific with an infectious laugh. She asked me if I would take an acid trip with her, which of course I did. Suddenly I found myself part of a band of drug smugglers bringing *charas* from the mountains and out of the country. We'd ride on the back of motorbikes driven by locals to score mushroom juice from Mushroom Jack, then go back to the beach and trip all day. From once watching Disney on acid I had now graduated to living it for real in an endless psychedelic *Jungle Book* complete with pulsating palm trees and imaginary tigers waiting to jump out at every corner. After a few days my beach hut was robbed, all my cash taken, and I spent the rest of my stay sharing Maria's hut on a pig farm. While I was with her I shaved off my hair, a symbolic rejection of corporate life before making my way back to London, already checked out from responsibility.

My resentment towards work had already grown out of control. A disagreement with Ken over a potential tax liability, which I blew out of all proportion, was the breaking point. I stormed off to 'work for myself', my path lit brightly only by the bridge I'd left burning behind me. In reality I sat in my flat for days on end, seething with injustice, feeling lost and useless. Without the regular hours and predictable structure of a working week, which I had resented for so long, I began to flounder. By day I trained to become a fitness instructor, pounding the studio floor, lifting weights to music, putting endless pressure on my joints, all for the sake of the perfect appearance. At night I skulked around the speed garage scene with my friend Steve, gazing at the reflection of angry teenagers smoking crack pipes, before we dived into a Vauxhall club to see out the rest of the night. And on one such cold February morning, to complete the rebellious picture, I attracted an ex-con, Will. Emerging from the shadows, he declared himself crazy for me and, right there and then, over a wrap of cocaine handed to me in the dirty toilet, I fell deeper and deeper into the mud of the lotus pond.

That mud was dark. It was thick. It was compelling. It sucked me down. For all my discomfort, every step took me further in. I had already walked away from a highly paid and responsible job so that I could smoke weed and watch Jerry Springer until lunchtime. Now, to top it all I was about to push myself through a tortuous cycle of pain and humiliation with another damaged soul.

A few years before I had been at a popular fetish club called the Torture Garden. Natasha and I would go there pretty regularly, but one night stands out in particular. It was a busy night, packed. Various floorshows were in full swing – quite extreme in some cases. In fact, everywhere I looked there was a lively scene of activity playing out before me. Natasha introduced me to a polite and handsome guy who told me he was an airline pilot. We chatted for a while before he asked me if I wanted to do anything. 'Yes' I said, 'I really want to hug.' He put his arm around me and I rested my head on his chest and then he just held me there for what seemed like hours. There we were, standing together in the middle of an orgy of sexual activity, just holding each other close. And for me it felt like the most intimate and erotic thing we could have done, considering our environment. A contradiction in my sexual expression was rapidly gaining momentum.

Addiction to Will was, in the most part, an addiction to sex. It was the sex that hooked me in, and it was the sex that kept me there. Sex with Will was everything I could have wanted. It felt like sex ought to. Strip away our differences, our incompatibility, our confusion, our problems, the sex between us was an intimate, honest and tender experience – and it melted my heart every time.

From the first kiss my heart rate flickered to attention,

a tingling sensation taking me by surprise, and then a slow beautiful ache that grew deep inside as I felt myself go moist in longing anticipation. His soft lips would take my mouth and kiss me a million times before working his way down to my breasts, which he caressed, my nipples sending electric currents through my body, which ached the more he kissed me. Will would go down on me for ages, sometimes making me come before he went inside me; sometimes teasing me for ages, holding me on the edge of an orgasm before making me come all over him as he went in deep.

It was the latter I preferred, feeling the closest union between us in that moment he entered. Once he was inside, he would just stay there, almost motionless, feeling the pulse between us. The closeness of this moment had always struck me as profound. An ultimate, godlike connection where the material world fades into insignificance. There is nothing more than this. Will naturally exploited it, holding us there for the longest time, always making me wonder how he was going to move, how he would take me this time. It was always different somehow. Was it him or me that I could feel throb that way? It was impossible to tell. In that moment, there was no separation between what was me and what was him.

I would tighten around him, holding him in as we both grew hotter, closer with each moment. He would talk to me then, sweet words, playing with my humour, sharing his pleasure. How he loved to be inside me. How it was the best. We hardly dared breathe, so tender was this moment. And then eventually, after sharing this perfect place for as long as we could dare, he would move inside me, perfectly timed, holding me at the brink of fulfillment until we burst all over each other and shouted out in shared ecstasy. Once we arrived we would often cry. Will sobbing first, and I completely understood why he would. Sometimes there were tears in our eyes before we came, just so moved by the intensity of the emotion between us. It was precious.

We took photographs. Intimate pictures that we worked on for hours. It was never cruel, never harsh, always gentle. He was the sweetest man in these times. The best playmate ever. We would laugh so much as we played our games. I was his sex slave for the day. Then he was mine. Sometimes he gave me a time limit to come. *You've got twenty seconds to come all over me. Go!*

Like that Torture Garden hug, Will and I were nothing extreme. Nothing sophisticated. Nothing outrageous. Sometimes he asked me to take him too and he came almost as soon as I did. No groups, no threesomes, very little bondage that I remember. Just straight up, one on one. Boy and girl, man and woman, sharing only with each other. But it was that feeling, when he was deep inside me that was like no other. That's what I was addicted to. That's the sexual feeling I had *always* been addicted to. That's what I could not leave. How could anything so beautiful possibly be wrong?

Had Will and I been even half the relationship out of the bedroom that we were in the bedroom, we probably could have lasted. But for the rest of our intimate life our differences were as extreme as the closeness of our physicality. It was neither appropriate nor healthy.

I gave it everything I had, using a toxic mix of sex and money to feed the beast, then immediately feeling used and unappreciated, my dissatisfaction stirring into perpetual indignation. I abandoned myself to this reality, painfully aware of how unhealthy it felt, but still somehow unable to walk away. The damage started to show physically. One morning I couldn't get out of bed. My back was in such agony that I could not walk away – quite literally. It took me two hours to get ten feet across the room to find my phone and call for help. Will and I argued endlessly. We never resolved anything. My anger was often stoked to the point that I would snap, sometimes throwing myself at him in a violent rage. When the dust had settled I would be exhausted, even more worn out than before. And still it felt like love.

Love?

Did I even know love?

What had happened during those formative years of my life, the years when I was supposed to learn what love is?

As addiction progressed, situations that had once been unpleasant began to border on dangerous. Will had a violent history and yet I provoked him, unable to step out of arguments or keep a cool head. Once I accidentally slammed a car door on my hand and passed out, unconscious from the pain. I woke up with Will shaking me desperately, my fingernail hanging off, blood everywhere. On a separate occasion he held a gun at my head, only as a joke, he said. It wasn't funny. And a holiday in Spain descended into a bust-up in our apartment, which ended with me hurling a glass of red wine at the wall. The smash broke the peace and tranquility of the Mediterranean hotel, and snapped one of the last remaining threads of affection between us. The red stain on the beautiful white wall was like blood shed. It was impossible.

In all of this I somehow managed to set up a business, a creative agency called, not surprisingly, Hyper. Steve found our first client and Peaches came to my place every day to work on the project and we got things off the ground. MyVillage.com hired us to do their PR. Then we found offices in Acton on the music-recording street, Warple Way. We won a contract with Capital Radio, and soon after, Polaroid. By March 2001, against all the odds, we were up and running. I had invested the last of my funds, forcing myself into a position where failure was not an option.

Things looked hopeful and we won a few more contracts. I employed staff, but I wasn't taking a salary and was living off the last of my savings. The slowdown was inevitable. The Internet bubble had burst. Sales became harder; cash flow was tight everywhere. I became an emotional bully, and Peaches took the brunt of it. I wasn't stable enough to carry the responsibility of owning a business. My addictions raged; the stress grew unbearable. After the glass-smashing holiday, I came back to London in despair.

Sara, my old friend from university days, lived in rural Derbyshire. Despite living in different parts of the country we had remained close, spending many weekends together, catching up and having good times. Yet although we were close I could never articulate what was really going on with me. I felt too ashamed.

Today Sara had given birth to twins, a boy called Callum and a girl called Ella. I drove up to see her. As I stepped into the gentle peacefulness of the maternity wing of a sweet countryside hospital, only hours after the birth, it was difficult to contemplate two more different lives than hers and mine. Yet Sara continued to welcome me into her life, and to my complete amazement asked me to be Ella's godmother. I was astonished. And deeply, most deeply honoured.

Holding Callum and Ella was a profound experience that I shall never forget. I was enthralled, captivated and intrigued. Callum fascinated me the most. He looked so old, like a tiny Benjamin Button, so wrinkled and with such an expression of profound concern and responsibility on his face that I felt he already carried the wisdom of a hundred-year-old man. Ella was just luminously beautiful. They both slept in my arms, and Sara told me how lucky she was to have me in her life, that I was her true sister. I felt our sisterhood that day. I was uplifted, despite all of the turmoil in my head. Only a sister could have shown such unreserved and unconditional love.

Back in London, however, as I turned the key in the front door each evening, all I could think about was dying. I had put on weight, and my skin was a mess. My thoughts were becoming more and more clouded and my self-esteem was on the floor. I knew that I was spiritually barren. I knew I was searching for something. What exactly, I did not know. Inner peace? Inner tranquility? Even in the most beautiful of environments it was me that seemed to spoil it. The disturbance was in my head. I was at odds with myself, and with the world.

Then, one day, out of the blue, I met Margie, in her clinic on Crawford Street. I was there for colonic irrigation; a solution I thought would free the physical energy that was so rigidly blocked. As I lay down for my treatment we started to talk. When I looked at Margie, this curious, seventy-year-old woman, I saw Yoda from *Star Wars*, and felt that I was in the presence of the wisest, oldest soul who knew everything of any importance that ever needed to be known. I started to tell her about myself, how I'd set up my own business, but how I was scared it would go under. Without hesitation she said,

'You should just chant through your fear.'

'Chant what?' I asked.

'Nam-myoho-renge-kyo.'

Something inside, other than the two litres of water swilling around my belly, moved.

'Say that again', I said. 'How do you say it?'

She repeated it slowly and I joined in.

'Nam. Myoho. Renge. Kyo. Nam. Myoho. Renge. Kyo.' I started to get my tongue around the words and repeated it until I was chanting the entire phrase. So yeah. My first Buddhist mantra was indeed chanted, lying on a bed with my knickers off and a hosepipe up my bum.

Enlightenment. Ah, the path to enlightenment…

Whatever I may have thought enlightenment was, this moment was certainly nothing like it. Had I been expecting a ray of light to descend from the heavens, casting me in a soft and rapturous glow, soothing me into peaceful contentedness, I would have probably ignored this spiritualized anal encounter and carried on regardless, continuing my search for a fix to all of life's sufferings. I didn't feel brightly illuminated or radically different. I was still me, the self-righteous, fearful, shameful person that had walked into that clinic with constipation an hour before. I still had my twenty carriages of emotional freight hauled behind me. I still had my life surrounding me, with all its complexities, its inauthenticity and its downright absurdity. But there was a difference. Unperceivable almost, but undeniably there.

I think of it now as a pilot light, ignited somewhere deep within my consciousness. Gently burning, gently alight, flickering and fragile. A low light, hardly warm and only just there. But there nevertheless. A light of compassion. A light of hope. I found that if I chanted the mantra I could somehow connect with that light and make it burn a little brighter. I could be more aware of it. It warmed me. It illuminated things inside my head. It vibrated gently. In my heart.

Peaches noticed the difference straight away. When I arrived at work the next morning, I confided for the first time that I needed to break things off with Will. Peaches burst out laughing and said how perfect it was that I had to get the shit taken out of me to lose Will too. Chanting gave me more energy. It made me look after myself better. I started juicing, caring about nutrition, getting my shit *together* if anything. Most significantly, my consciousness rose. I started to notice things that previously I had either ignored or failed to see, although they had been there for years, right under my nose. This wasn't necessarily easy. In fact, if anything, I started to see how appalling things actually were and how appalling I could be. In these moments it was like when you've seen it out to the bitter end in a nightclub and all the lights go on, or the moment you walk outside and it's cold, bright daylight and you are completely wasted. A kind of spiritual *Time Please!* that had me staring into the mirror of my soul. What I saw reflected back was so difficult I could hardly bear to look.

I would still smoke joints to switch off, soothing myself under a temporary blanket of delusion. But all the time that damn pilot light kept on burning away at the back of my consciousness, just a little bit stronger each time I chanted. Gently reminding me that any number of joints were never going to take away my suffering. Bit by bit old survival strategies were being hung out to dry, a pitiful line of washed-out time-faded habits that I couldn't yet manage to take down, even though I knew I needed to throw them out completely.

In a moment of weakness, one warm and sunny Sunday afternoon, I drove over to Will's place. I was angry before I arrived and it only took a few minutes before I was ranting and raving about something that had upset me. This particular episode was prolonged and possibly the loudest and most frustrated of all. I ran across the living room, throwing myself at Will with everything I'd got, screaming at him in desperation. Across the peacefulness of the estate, someone shouted *Shut the fuck up!* It was shameless. I sat on the floor shaking, my temples pounding, my head between my knees now, sobbing with the realization that I had become… my father.

Will urged me to talk to my parents. And he was right. I needed to resolve this with them, not him. It was an early Sunday evening. Normally they would have been at church. But when I dialled their number, not only did my mother pick up the phone, my father also picked up the second handset at exactly the same time. They both said *Hello?* in unison. I could hardly speak for sobbing.

'Ruth, is that you?'

'Yes.'

'What's happened?'

'Remember the rage attacks that Dad used to have? Well, I'm having them too.'

'Yes. We know.'

It was a turning point. It was the moment I started to take responsibility for my life. I started to see how it didn't matter what anyone else had done to me, past or present, I was the only person that could change anything now. It all came down to me. I walked away from Will and sat in meditation for hours, chanting to connect with my greater self, my deeper consciousness, my wisdom, compassion and courage. If I were to stand a chance of changing anything, I needed more wisdom, compassion and courage than I could possibly ever imagine.

And I reflected on something Margie had said:

Forgiving the people who gave you life and who hurt you at the same time is one of the most difficult things to do. But the lotus flower that has its roots in the darkest muddiest pond is the lotus flower that blooms the biggest and the brightest.

Peaches and I took a trip to Dublin to train with our software partner. We shared a hotel room, reminiscent of our party days in Madrid, where we'd always crashed in her bed together. Now we were working women, serious and business-focused. In the morning, as we watched the breakfast news, it struck me that it wasn't just me that was in turmoil; it was the world. The news showed men and women physically throwing themselves at Eurotunnel trains, so desperate were they to cross the UK border. People were literally dying to get into our recession-bleak country. Three days later, back now in our London office, someone rushed in to tell us about a plane crash in New York. And as that day unfolded, so did the events of September 11, 2001. The day it came to a head. When it all came to light. The incandescent anger of two parties in conflict. Fall out. To the extreme.

On 12 September Louise called.

'Are you sitting down, Ruth?'

'I'm driving, so yes.'

'The plane crash in New York... Graham was on the second plane.'

'What?!'

No, no, no, no, no. Please, please. No.

The brilliant Graham. The kind Graham. The entertaining Graham. The generous and talented Graham. I had been longing to tell him about my meditation discoveries, inspired by his own practice – a practice he'd told me about only two years earlier, on a trip to Napa Valley. Graham, Louise and me. Now he was murdered, his precious life ripped away from him as he'd made his journey from Boston to Los Angeles. Louise was waiting expectantly for him – a significantly expectant time for her as she carried her first baby, due in December.

We considered the last hour of Graham's life. No, he hadn't tried to call from the plane. He'd been in good spirits that morning as he left for the airport, excited to see Louise and her baby bump later that day. He was on Flight 175, the plane that crashed into the second tower of the World Trade Centre. The same crash that was so clearly filmed, its image replayed again and again and once more again, the most memorable footage of 9/11 as it seared into the retina of a generation, changing the world as we knew it.

Grief, loss and injustice. Not just staring us in the face now, but driving a dagger deep into our hearts.

And there was I. Looking at my life, with all the bridges I had burned, the arguments I had taken one step too far, the conflicts I had caused or failed to resolve, and the loves that I had lost. With my anger burning, I looked out at a world illuminated by the flames of an argument that, until this moment, we hadn't even known about. And of course the sickening thought of the inevitable retaliation that ricocheted back in a heartbeat. More violence. More bloodshed. More loss of human life. And for what? For peace? This wasn't the peace I wanted to feel in my heart or see in the world. I had to do something different. There had to be better way.

I knelt down and chanted to take responsibility for my life. I chanted for the desire to change myself and change my world. I chanted for all of those who had passed away that day, and then for every single person who had lost their life through war or violence. I chanted for my deceased relatives who had gone before me. I chanted for Paul S, for Kenny, for John, for William, for Andrew, for Alberto, for everyone. And above all today I chanted for Graham Andrew Berkeley, 12 January 1964–11 September 2001. And then I prayed for peace throughout the whole world and for the happiness of all humanity, because I wish for another what I wish for myself. It was time to change this world for the better, starting with me.

This world needs peace.

I want peace.

Let's roll!

Chapter Five

Tranquility

If you care anything about your personal security, you should first of all pray for order and tranquility throughout the four quarters of the land, should you not?

On Establishing the Correct Teaching
for the Peace of the Land[1]

It was a golden day in the tropics. I sat on a deserted beach of coral sand shimmering in the heat, mesmerized by the waves breaking on the shore only a few feet away. The water swelled in a powerful rhythm, back and forth, the colours refracting indigo and turquoise before exploding with bubbles of light as the waves gently curled and crashed down. The sky was the brightest, deepest blue that it ever gets, unblemished by any clouds above the horizon. The hot sun bathed my skin, warming it like melted chocolate. The sea breeze, also warm, soothed my senses. A deep calm settled into my bones. Everything was OK. I was exactly where I wanted to be – a peaceful place after the endless chaos and turmoil. Tranquility at last.

I'd sat on this beautiful beach for a week now, looked after by a simple, hardworking family who owned a few beach huts on the seashore. The journey from Colombo airport had taken five hours by car, winding and swinging its way along an ever-narrowing road. The place was remote. And I was alone. When I'd finally reached the humble shack on Christmas Eve, I'd sat on the porch, slightly shocked at the immensity of the step I'd taken, breathing in the sounds and sights of Sri Lanka. Monkeys ran across the straw roof of my hut, birdcalls I'd only ever heard in the zoo rose up, and then the constant sound of the Indian Ocean crashing rhythmically in the background. At first my heart shook with fear and loneliness. I had expected this. Yet I knew deep down this was exactly where I needed to be.

It was the chanting that had brought me here, of course. Not to this geographical place in particular, but on this journey, away from the cold and dark to spend Christmas on my own, far away from everything. The more I'd chanted, the more clearly I'd seen how disturbed my mind was. By adjusting the lens everything came into focus. The chaos was clear. *But how to change things? Where to start?*

I'd chanted every day. I'd studied. I'd listened to experienced practitioners and taken their words to heart. That Buddhism was about transformation. That everyone has the capacity for wisdom, compassion and courage, the precious qualities of the Buddha. That our current circumstances are the vehicles for transforming the negative stuff and bringing out these qualities. That this process of changing things – they called it 'human revolution' – is how we become happy. That all the drugs, the unsuccessful relationships, the business struggles, the angry tirades – these mattered to no one. On the contrary, they were the perfect conditions for revealing my happiness. That all I had to do was practise sincerely so that wisdom, compassion and courage would naturally arise. It was a simple, non-judgmental equation that my new teachers revealed. I could, I really *could*, change my life.

And so I chanted. And read. And listened.

Good effects came quickly, which motivated me to continue. A few business contracts came in unexpectedly. My health improved. I had more energy. There was a better atmosphere in the office. Yet for all the apparent simplicity of the practice it was not easy. There was a lot to change. After that shameless Sunday afternoon fight with Will had come the deep-set grief of another failed relationship. Moreover, taking responsibility for my anger was humiliating and difficult. Now the whole world was stunned by the shock of 9/11, which, aside from collective grief, had sent financial markets into free fall and a global red alert across the world that set the prevailing moodometer at F-E-A-R.

Wallowing in despair and self-pity late one Friday evening, I was startled by a friend from the office next door who found me staring at the computer, head in hands. After listening to my tale of woe for five minutes, she found the Sri Lankan beach hut online. Within days I had booked a flight. It was both terrifying and exciting.

On the empty beach I was exposed to all the elements, but I was protected too. First of all I had no desire for alcohol or drugs. Not one bit. The mother of the family who owned the huts cooked me one meal a day on her wood fire. It was vegetarian and it was the best food I had ever tasted. I was given fruit for breakfast and if I asked for a biscuit or a cake she laughed at me and said 'No!'

I was encouraged to take a daily massage from a doctor who practised close by in a clinic across a small lagoon that could only be reached by boat. The first time I went, a local boy took me there. He told me to take off my clothes and get on the table, and even though he wasn't the doctor, I reluctantly did as he asked, not sure where this was going. His hands were dirty and felt rough on my skin, and I could tell that he was an imposter. I told him to get off and go away. When the real doctor arrived and found out what had happened he was really upset. To make up for it, he gave me a massage every day with his proper assistant helping. It was the first time I had been massaged like this, with hot oil and special ayurvedic herbs, and it was exactly what my body needed. It bordered on euphoric as the aches and pains and the toxins melted away. I slept so soundly in my hut each night, my dreams vivid and clear, and awoke each morning to a different level of consciousness.

I made friends with the eldest son of the family. He took me out in the sea he knew so well, navigating the rocks and currents and showing me where it was safe to swim. One night we walked for miles down the beach under a full moon, looking for turtles coming out of the water to lay their eggs. We didn't see any, but I'll never forget the beach that night, illuminated in silver by the moon, with the phosphorescent waves crashing on the shore. When we got back to the dwelling my friend offered me a beer. I declined and went up to my hut. Although it was after midnight I was baking hot from the long walk, so I stripped off before having a shower. As I came back into the room I saw, out of the corner of my eye, the curtain at the window, hovering. It was being lifted up with a stick! *Someone was peeping!* I froze for a second, and then screamed at the top of my voice for the whole community to hear. There were noises underneath the window as someone ran away. Eventually the eldest son, my friend, came up. A lame search of the grounds revealed no one. There were no trespassers. The dogs had not stirred. It dawned on me, months later, that it was probably him at my window. For all my wild days and crazy past, I could be so incredibly naive. These boys could (and still do, for better or worse) see me coming.

The best thing about this magical week was undoubtedly the time I devoted to my unfolding Buddhist practice. I woke early and chanted as the sun rose on the east side of the beach; and in the evening as it set on the west side. During the day I studied a book which explained the theory and the chanting practice in exhilarating depth. Its author, Richard Causton, who'd passed away a few years earlier, had discovered Buddhism whilst serving in the British army and travelling in the Far East. His experience was personal and full of integrity and made absolute sense to me. This was a philosophy I had instinctively known since childhood. Rather than a fantasy or a nirvana that could never be reached, what he described was based on real life and actual proof. And when I came to the part that explains the perspective on life and death, I felt a sense of absolute clarity:

> *The Buddhist concept of the eternity of life places the life of the individual in the context of the universe as a whole, asserting that since the entire universe exists in one form or another throughout eternity, so must all living things contained within it exist eternally in one form or another. Thus no living thing can either be created or destroyed. What appears to be creation and destruction is, in reality, simply the power of renewal, inherent in the limitless life force of the universe at work in an ever changing variety of forms, like a huge kaleidoscope; neither is this process random but follows the unending cycle of birth, maturation, decline and death according to the law of the universe.*[2]

In wonder, I read the passage again. I had never heard life and death described in this way before. Most religions or philosophies view death from one of two extremes: one as annihilation – that is, when you are dead you are dead; and the other as permanence – that your soul or spirit continues unchanging into the afterlife. The Buddha considered both these views, although widely held, not helpful. He believed that the thought of annihilation creates anxiety and fear around death, and that a permanent view strengthens self-attachment and therefore deepens people's delusion. Instead, he proposed the Middle Way, a new way of perceiving the constantly changing nature of our lives.

Now I was hooked. What was this Middle Way?

> *Our lives exist, have always existed, and will always exist simultaneously with the universe. They neither came into*

being before the universe, occurred accidentally, nor were they created by a supernatural being... Life and death are the alternating aspects in which our real self manifests itself, and both are part of the cosmic essence.[3]

The waves crashed on the shore in front of me. Their rhythmic ebb and flow transfixed me and I felt at one with the earth's elements:

Myoho refers to this eternal rhythm of life and death.[4]

I paused, soaking in the sun along with the idea:

If you imagine the life force of the universe as the ocean, an individual can be likened to a single wave on the surface of the ocean. From this it follows that the single wave is in no way different to the rest of the ocean around it. The only factor that gives it a momentary identity is its physical form by which, for a short space of time, it appears defined as a wave with its own unique behaviour and characteristics. The wave that is seen at the surface is merely a product of the forces and energies of a larger wave motion existing unseen within the ocean. Strictly speaking, then, we could speak of the 'seen' wave deriving from the 'unseen' wave. Finally, the concentration of the kinetic energy, which originally created the 'seen' wave from the 'unseen' wave, will, after a time, become dissipated, and so the 'seen' wave will collapse, merging once more into the deep 'unseen' waves of the ocean from which it appeared. In other words, at death, our life does not physically go anywhere because it is already concomitant with the universe. Although at death our form and consciousness no longer function, the entity of our life itself continues in the same way that the wave motion continues, unseen in the depths of the ocean after the seen wave at the surface has collapsed.[5]

I breathed in the warm air and watched the waves breaking. The scene had a beauty and clarity I'd never experienced before. And in that moment, I understood. I felt connected with my greater self, the beating pulse of life and death.

Here was an awakening far different from the stirring in my belly a few months before on Margie's table. This was an awakening that felt profound, indelible. And for all of life's ups and downs since then, nothing has shaken it. It was a life-affirming, peaceful moment that I always think back to, including in my darkest hours. From that day on, I knew there was a different way to live.

As I sat there, contemplating this idea that the essence of an individual's life is not extinguished after death, I began to reflect on the lives of my ancestors, the genetic waves of previous generations from which my own life had emerged – the unseen forces that move beneath the surface until the conditions are right for new life to appear. That's how our lives continue, through the generations, through the centuries, through the ages.

I remembered two figures in particular, two people with whom I'd felt an over-riding sense of security and unconditional love as a child: my paternal grandfather, Albert, and my maternal grandmother, Irene. What was our deep connection? Where did they and I forge our energetic links of life?

My grandfather, Albert, was the son of a Sheffield postman called Leonard and his wife Annie. There are no pictures of his parents – they were too poor ever to be photographed. And no record of his grandparents whatsoever. When Leonard passed away, Annie was completely heartbroken. She died in a local mental hospital of something they termed 'melancholia'. I thought of Annie, of her heartache, and of my own times of depression and romantic trauma, her unseen waves of emotional longing resonating strongly with my life.

Albert married a girl called Mildred, whose own father had

died when she was young, leaving her mother, Lily, to battle through life on her own. She had been the beneficiary of a large life insurance policy on his death, but a local man convinced her to sign it into his name and he took the money for himself. Lily was distraught. After an intense fight she managed to get this man to pay her just enough to live on – but it was an absurdly small sum of what was actually her money. Lily lived with Albert and Mildred from when they married, and it is said that she had terrible problems with her temper, often raging in her unhappiness, lashing out at her daughter Mildred and her grandson, my father.

My father, David, was born in 1939. One year later Albert was called up to serve in the Second World War, leaving behind his wife, his mother-in-law and his small son to face the Sheffield blitz without him. I'm sure this troubled him greatly. It certainly traumatised my father, who apparently spent many nights in air-raid shelters, calling out in fear for his absent father's protection. A childhood wound that was never to heal.

Albert was shipped to Poona in India where he was assessed for battle. His eyesight was so poor that he couldn't fire at a target to save his life, let alone take someone else's, so he was put in charge of managing the petrol dump in what was to become India's foremost military hub. For three years he was stationed there and it was during these same three years that Gandhi was also held in Poona. Gandhi's wife died there and her ashes are interred in the grounds of the palace where they stayed. My grandfather must have lived only yards away.

When Albert returned from India he worked at Sheffield University for many years until his retirement in 1975. He had a deep Christian faith and practised what he preached. I remember a plaque on the fireplace that read *PRAYER CHANGES THINGS*. Grandad always encouraged me to pray about life's challenges. Was this the source of his positive and upbeat attitude? Certainly, his great energy and zest for life made him very popular. He never criticised anyone and rarely gave in to a negative view of people or circumstances. I loved going to visit him as a child because he would always make me laugh. He called me Toothless Ruthless when I was losing my baby teeth. When we went for country walks, he would pull me along on my roller skates, pandering to my love of movement and speed. On my ninth birthday, the year of junior school hell, he bought me my first piano music book and I practised devotedly every day so I that I could play for him. Everything I did met with his approval and encouragement. I must have been the apple of his eye.

Grandad loved the Yorkshire and Derbyshire countryside and was fit from walking the hills and vales. When he retired, he joined a rambling club and would talk excitedly about where he had been on his recent walks. One day he was mowing the lawn when he had a heart attack. Grandma got him straight to hospital. My father went to see him, coming home with news that recovery had already started. A few days later, however, after we'd travelled the familiar well-worn M1 route between Derby and Sheffield, my Grandmother received word from the hospital. Dad went with her while Mum, Mark, Matthew and I waited back at their apartment. Some time later Mum answered the phone and started to cry. This was my first experience of death, and my heart felt like it broke in two.

Only one person could console me. Later that day we made our way to see my mother's parents, and Nan, my maternal grandmother, saved my heart. While the family sat in the living room, drinking tea and saying very little, without a word Nan took me upstairs to her bedroom and lay me down on the bed next to her. I was intoxicated with that familiar sweet smell of her beautiful room. She spoke in the softest, kindest tones. She told me that I was very special to Grandad, that he loved me very much, and that he was safe and happy. There was something extraordinary in the way she comforted me. It worked.

Now as I gazed out across the Indian Ocean, contemplating this man that I had loved and lost as a child. I thought, too, of the book's author, Richard Causton. He had also served in the British Army and travelled to the East. I wondered if he and my grandfather had ever met each other in India. It wasn't impossible, Poona being what it was to the British Forces at that time. Maybe they had shared a conversation together over tea in the Barracks? Maybe they had discussed their views on life, on war, on peace?

Looking out to the horizon, I sensed the energy of these two deceased veterans of war and their lives pulsating in the shifting watery expanse. I held them both in my heart. Grandad's love was already imprinted there. Richard Causton's words spoke to more than my intelligence; just like Nan's words on the day that Grandad passed away.

Nan.

Irene. My mother's mother.

Her bright blue eyes twinkled when she laughed. While strong and authoritative, she was incredibly feminine. Whenever she spoke everyone listened. Most of the time she was sweet and humorous, but when she put her foot down you knew it. Born into abject poverty in 1921, Nan was brought up by her grandparents alongside her cousin Laura. Later on, her father took his own life by drowning in a local reservoir. He left his peaked cap sitting on a rock. It was tragic.

At the beginning of the war Irene had been engaged to an RAF pilot called Kenneth, who was sent to serve in Canada, while she worked at Newton Chambers in Chapeltown. Her life, it seemed, was set. In Kenneth's absence, however, she fell in love with my Grandpa, a factory inspector, and they conceived my mother – a sequence of events she carried throughout her life without a murmur. No one else talked about it either; I realized it only when their fortieth wedding anniversary arrived and my mother's fortieth birthday fell six months later.

Years later my mother's sister, Aunt Sue, disclosed a romantic secret about Nan. To the day she died, Nan kept a list of all the occasions she and Kenneth had met before he went to war. One of their love trysts – and this left me speechless – had taken place at the very same hotel in Morecambe where I had lived during my second year at university! Another story of unrequited love had threaded its way through the generations of our family.

Love.

Love was always at stake.

These waves, this kinetic energy that we share, this pulse that connects us. How close we all are to each other. How our energies collide and glide beneath the surface and then above to where we co-exist. How connected we all are as we live and die together. Sometimes we meet a person for the first time, yet immediately sense a strong energetic connection. They seem familiar, as if we have known them before. Possibly we have. Who can fathom the nature of our relationship to them in lifetimes before this one?

When I was eighteen I was told that I looked like Irene's sister Thelma, who had died when she was twenty-one. And out of all of us, my brothers and my cousin, I was the one who inherited Nan's bright blue eyes. When I lived in that hotel room in Morecambe (maybe the very same bedroom where my Nan had stayed), Orlando would sing New Order, *Oh you've got green eyes, oh you've got blue eyes, oh you've got grey eyes.*[6] It is true. My eyes change colour depending on my mood, the weather and sometimes the hour.

Time spent with Nan as a child was blissful. She was the Fairy Queen and I was the Princess. It didn't matter what we were doing, she always gave me a sense of peace and tranquility. Nan taught me to play cards and we bet for matchsticks or pennies – Stop the Bus, Rummy and Whist. My happiest moments were curled up on the sofa with my head in her lap, watching old movies on TV: *It's a Wonderful Life*, *Breakfast at Tiffany's*, *National Velvet*, *Half a Sixpence* and of course *The Wizard of*

Oz. Sometimes I would drift off to sleep, while the sound of the old grandfather clock ticked reassuringly in the hallway.

Nan had great antiques. She collected fine bone china, especially limited editions. There was always something precious to look at. She had a magical jewellery box which we would go through for hours. She said that one day everything in it would belong to me. As I grew older we saw it through the rough times when I was deep in the grip of addiction, upsetting the family. When I met Gina, Nan was supportive – *I always thought it was a good idea to stick with the girls.* My later choices went down less well, and Nan made no attempt to hide her disapproval of my girlfriends after Gina. On her eightieth birthday when I turned up late, stoned and with ex-gangster in tow, I think she must have given up on the idea of me ever settling down with a suitable mate, male or female. I can't say that my issues didn't affect our relationship, but one thing I know for sure is that Nan was one of the people in my life, especially in my childhood, who showed me unconditional love. The fact that she did was my saving grace.

Love was there with my parents too. Sitting in peaceful reflection, I was able to connect back to the affirming times from my childhood, the nurturing bond I had with my parents, which, amidst all the turmoil, *did* exist. We suffered together in our shared pain and awkward embarrassment, but love still held us together in a precarious, sometimes contradictory relationship – a fragile meeting place of conflicting emotions where shamefulness often won over our shared hope for a happy life.

When we were children our family would go on holiday, once a year, during the summer break. Dad, being a school teacher, had six weeks off, and for at least three of these we would pack a tent into the car and head to some far-flung part of the British Isles for a usually damp and very occasionally scorching trip on the coast. We upgraded to a caravan in my early teens, but I slept in the awning. For me, summer holiday meant being under canvas.

As a young child I had adored my mother, but as I grew into my angry teens, our relationship broke down. I know that she feared what I might say or do next. Yet I remember one day being completely at peace with her on a beach at sunset. We sat on a rock together, basking in the warmth of a late August sun, which had lost its fierceness and now left us glowing. I wish I could remember what we talked about, what wisdom she had imparted to me as we sat there in our elusive mother-daughter union. Maybe it doesn't matter, because in that moment I felt absolutely connected with her. Connected with myself too. I knew who I was. Like when we ate fish and chips at the end of a day, our family of five lined up, perched on a seafront bench, chomping our food from the newspaper wrapper, sated by the taste of this salty, greasy heaven. Contented. Unified. At one.

Generations past and generations to come. The Buddha taught that what we do in the present moment can affect the lives of all our relatives, including our past and future ancestors. As I reflected on the deep and often painful connection with my parents I saw how our lives could be viewed in the context of our shared karma, the past and present causes that we'd made collectively and as individuals, which had brought us to where we now were:

> *The Contemplation of the Mind Sutra says, 'If you want to understand the causes that existed in the past, look at the results as they are manifested in the present. And if you want to understand what results will be manifested in the future, look at the causes that exist in the present.*[7]

Karma is not about retribution, or sin or fate or damnation. It is an affirmation of power and presence – and the potential to change. Misfortune can be transformed into good fortune.

How much more positive life becomes if we can believe this. Rather than aspiring for immortality in an eternally perfect world once we have died, if we can see the world in which we live as our *true* world, we can then take actions every day to make it a happy one, not just for ourselves but for others too. That's all that changing karma means.

With a fledging knowledge formulating in my mind I began to feel empowered. A sense of connection. A sense of belonging. Of course what we do in our present moment will change the lives of our ancestors, the lives of all of those that have come before us. We know we are connected. Our shared karma, our shared energy has proved this to us already. And so we can affect all life by changing our own.

Shafts of sunlight hit the surface of the ocean making it sparkle like a million jewels. A sea bird swooped down low, catching the breeze and then gliding up high. I picked up a handful of warm sand. As I let it run through my fingers, I made a promise to my grandfather that from this day on I would make him proud of me. And I promised my great-grandmothers that I refused to die of a broken heart or be bullied into poverty by anyone. It was a pact that I made with myself, not only for my sake, but also for the love of my family, past and present.

Eternity is now.

My awakening that glorious sunny day in Sri Lanka helped ground me securely on my new path towards happiness. It was a bright ray of light after a long path of despair. I smiled at everyone. Everyone smiled back. Isn't this all anyone needs to be content? Good health, food and shelter, and peace, with no one threatening to take what is theirs or hurt those they love. *This is humanity,* I thought.

How could I take this feeling back to London, to the life that I had constructed? My environment there was based on so much illusion and pretence and fear, it was difficult to know where to begin. Even my closest friends were not fully aware of my inner turmoil, nor me of theirs. I had acquired too many of the trappings of success even to feel my own pain, let alone share it with others. The challenge now was to make the changes in my life to become truly happy, to live freely and fulfilled.

If tranquility were the answer I could have sold up and moved to Sri Lanka forever, traded my London place for a beach hut, read good books and chanted, sold coconuts and seashells to put food on the table. But this is not the truth of life. We need a deeper power to withstand impermanence. We need a deeper power to help withstand the sufferings of sickness, old age, and death. Even for that wonderful family who lived such inspiring and generous lives. Their world was soon to be destroyed when the 2004 tsunami went crashing into their beach and swept them away.

Life changes. Sea changes. And the waves go deep.

Chapter Six

Rapture

Suffer what there is to suffer, enjoy what there is to enjoy. Regard both suffering and joy as facts of life and continue chanting Nam-myoho-renge-kyo, no matter what happens. Strengthen the power of your faith more than ever.

Happiness in This World[1]

Rapture. Enlightenment. What is the difference?

Rapture feels so great that at the time it can be deceiving. An ecstatic force of positivity that wells up inside making us feel happy to be alive. But what happens next – that's not always so pretty.

My time on the beach in Sri Lanka was rapturous as my health improved and the stresses of London seemed to melt away. I left Tungalle on a natural high, flying back overnight and landing on New Year's Day, vibrant, happy and hopeful. Nothing, I felt, could stop me now. *Bring it on!*

But rapture is not absolute. Rapture is not freedom. And rapture is not for ever. It comes and it goes. And when it goes it often gives way to a lower life state such as anger, hunger or even hell. In short, rapture is conditional. It depends on the fulfilment of desires. It seduces and it deludes. This is why, of all the life states, it is rapture that I fear the most.

Hedonism had never really been a good lifestyle option for me.

A happy hedonist, I believe, is robust enough to roll with the comedowns. Splash cold water on their face and carry on. They have a firm grip on who they are. I did not. As a result, my life had become a catalogue of short-lived highs followed by often embarrassing, and sometimes heartbreaking, bewildering disappointments. Ecstatic moments sharply ending left my heart torn and my sense of self a bit more ragged each time.

Yet still I believed in a fairy-tale fantasy where love would save the day. A strong young man would fall in love with me, rescue me from the injustices and evils of the world and we would live happily ever after. A bit like *The Little Mermaid*, I guess: the Walt Disney version at least (a particular favourite of mine, usually on LSD, back in the day).

The original story of *The Little Mermaid*, written by the Danish author Hans Christian Andersen in 1837, is altogether darker and far more challenging. In this, our Little Mermaid lives in a beautiful palace at the bottom of the sea but she longs to live on land as a human. Unlike mermaids, she had been told, humans possess a soul that continues to the afterlife. One day, as the Little Mermaid ventures to the sea's surface, a handsome prince passes by. She falls in love at first sight. Desperate to be with him, she makes a pact with a sea witch and exchanges her beautiful voice for a pair of human legs and a huge amount of pain. For she must charm the prince by dancing for him, and every step she takes will feel like daggers in the bottom of her feet. Everything hinges on the prince accepting her as his wife. If he does not, she will die a mermaid's death and her soul will perish.

Her plan works, to the point that the prince does indeed fall in love with her. But without a voice our mute heroine is unable to express herself, and an unfortunate string of events leads to the prince marrying the 'wrong girl', therefore sealing the mermaid's fate. The sea witch offers her life back in the ocean if she will slay the prince with a sword; but instead she chooses self-sacrifice. After the Little Mermaid dies, the 'gods' concede that her soul shall be sustained only if she carries out good deeds for all those on earth. And so, unlike her tragically unfulfilled earthly desires, the Little Mermaid's immortality is finally granted.

Hans Christian Andersen's nineteenth-century tale was clearly designed to scare his young readers – especially any girl who wanted to stray beyond the confines into which she had been born. It was also a condemnation of desires and longings, which can end only in suffering and unrequited love. Could this depressing story be any further from the tale of the Dragon King's Daughter, the eight-year-old girl from the *Lotus Sutra* who transformed into a Buddha? The latter, with its promises of hope and freedom and enlightenment, was yet to be discovered in Europe when Andersen penned his tale of gloom. Even since then, the gloriously animated 1989 Disney version is a clichéd interpretation of romantic love, the heroine's happiness secured only by a prince, on whom she must depend.

With twenty-first-century hindsight, I now see *The Little Mermaid* as a story of pure unadulterated love addiction. Looking to love as the fix for her unhappiness, our Little Mermaid acts out the archetypal irrational moves and traumatic self-sacrifice that any 'self-disrespecting' sex and love addict knows all too well. And it was my own search for enlightenment in a rapturous world of romance that nearly sealed my own fate. Only by drawing from the wisdom of the *Lotus Sutra* would I eventually find where true happiness lay.

'Chant for your heart's desires', the Buddhists told me.

For me, only love was the answer.

Always love.

I had met Hermione a year earlier when she was singing in a club in Notting Hill. The place was buzzing that night. All the beautiful people were there and the mood was high. Hermione stood out with her confidence, her extraordinary vocals and her sassy sense of entitlement to the limelight. We were introduced, and instantly captivated, caught up in animated conversation, suddenly blind to our respective lovers, both of us exhilarated by our rare and easy connection.

A year later, now both single, our friendship took off. Night after night on the phone, talking endlessly about our hopes and dreams or hanging out at her place while she produced music. Loving her company, loving just being there. Her smile was radiant. She lit up my life. Stars exploded like fairy dust when she shook her long locks of hair, and she laughed from a place where angels sang. I was caught in her spell. It was sublime.

What could I give this perfect creature? How could I prove my love?

I offered to support her career; I offered help with her son; I promised everything. We set sail on a rapturous sea of music, gigs, events, parties and holidays. At home we slipped into domestic bliss, never more than a few feet apart. I felt an incredible sense of possibility and optimism. Here in Hermione must be the love I had chanted for. I would commit all my resources, emotional, physical and material, to making sure that this love would last.

I stretched my finances to buy us a home. Our house parties would start with two cases of *Veuve* in the fridge, a DJ in the corner, and fifty people up for a good time; they would end with ten of us in the bathtub for Sunday brunch. Most of the time, though, we were domestic. Hermione was a responsible mother and I took on the mantle of being a second parent with all the seriousness I could muster. That was part of the problem. The fantasy of being a conscientious step-parent was far from its tricky reality.

Living with each other was the start of the decline. At first it was a carousel ride, a happy musical merry-go-round with pretty horses and warm flickering lights. We laughed together, clinging to each other in giddy excitement. But when the arguments began, the carousel horses morphed into bumper cars, boisterously jabbing at each other, then spinning around in stomach-churning circles. We began to call it the 'misery go round' because each time it went full circle we were just a little bit more fractious than before. And yet we couldn't get off. We just kept going for one more misery-go-round time.

Addictive relationships are difficult to fathom. As much as Hermione and I felt a powerful connection, we also felt destined to fail. We wrangled with each other, completely enmeshed yet at the same time desperate to pull away. We took it in turns to be either the 'dependent one' or the 'get-the-fuck-out-of-here one'. We danced, like the Little Mermaid, on knives.

Our arguments began to escalate into full-blown rows when her son was staying with his father. Once I flirted with the idea of seeing someone else. When Hermione got wind, she threw my mobile phone to the floor, not realizing that my foot was in the way. It hit me so hard that it left a bright purple bruise all the way from the top of my foot to the bottom of my sole. It looked like I had been shot. This is what love addiction feels like. This is what love addiction is. Shooting yourself in the foot.

At work I found it hard to concentrate, often turning up in tears, distressed about what was happening at home. Financially I was starting to panic. So much time and money had gone into 'Project Hermione' that I'd become unfocused. Our spending was out of control. We were not living within our means.

I chanted for an investor in the business and unbelievably within days one appeared. When a Canadian company took over our software provider, the new CEO, let's call him 'Mr. Steal', proposed that we should become their UK office. A posh British man backed him: 'Mr. Deal' played on his lineage to the royal family, taking me on a private tour of his father-in-law's stately home and grounds. Then they shipped in the Gay Girl, their Vancouver-based 'lawyer', a witty and attractive lesbian who flattered me each time we met. Becoming part of this new team was like meeting Hermione two years earlier. It felt like a change in fortune, which again I naturally credited to my chanting. Now my business was part of a larger company, which would float within a year and turn my shares to gold.

After signing the purchase agreement and seduced by the high life, I lived the dream for a while, flying between meetings in hip hotels in Toronto, Vancouver, New York and Seattle. Mr. Deal introduced me to First Class, and for a while I was happy to endure sleepless nights listening to his snoring as we chugged across the Atlantic. It soon lost its appeal when Friday night flights replaced my usual Saturday morning lie-in with a British Airways' breakfast sandwich in a business class cabin full of farting, hung-over businessmen.

Alcohol and drugs had taken the back seat now, chipping into my consciousness occasionally like two unsettled children: 'Are we nearly there yet?' In the front it was finance and romance that battled for the driving seat, arguing like two codependent lovers who could neither live with nor without each other. Rapture? It was not. I knew I was on course for a crash.

At home things were only getting worse. A holiday in Mauritius with Hermione at the end of 2004 was the beginning of the end. A last-ditch attempt to save our hopeless relationship. We were in paradise and we were in hell. How could something that had been so hopeful, so wonderful, become so hard? I thought of all the effort, everything I had done, how much I had given for the sake of this love. How I had failed at every turn. And now we were as far apart as we had once been close.

I reflected on this at sunset one evening, taking a walk alone to find some space. As I looked out across the beach I felt the earth begin to shake beneath my feet. I fell down hard. Later we found out that the biggest tsunami on record had swept across the Indian Ocean killing thousands of people. On a tidal wave of grief and devastation Hermione and I faced the truth. Our romance was over.

At first I looked to my work for relief, but here too I was powerless. The new owners were not credible leaders, and their lack of ethics quickly became apparent. They wanted me to promote their strategy by proxy, to do their dirty work, such as firing staff or approaching potential investors or partners with inflated claims about our resources. I should have walked away, but I was swept along on a rushing tide of denial.

They sent me a letter one day, 'Steal and Deal', accusing me of fraud and dismissing me from the business. They stopped my pay. They cut me off from the bank. They even stopped my phone. They told my colleagues in London not to speak to me. I was paralysed. Just like the Little Mermaid who had sacrificed her tongue, I had no voice. I'd been too busy trying to find myself in a world of success, of status, and love.

When I told a friend what had happened, he went pale:

'You're telling me that pretty much the worse thing that could happen to your career has just happened', he said. 'What are you going to do?'

'Change my karma.' I said.

What else could I do?

I chanted with a determination I had never mustered before. *Fight for justice*, the voice inside of me said. *Find your voice. Stand up for yourself.* That would mean going through six months of litigation. So be it. I was resolute. I had to believe in myself. I learned a lot during those months. I saw how dirty people would play. I saw how I set myself up for exploitation. I saw the nature of my delusion. And I also experienced the courage and compassion of two extraordinary women.

Only one person stood by me at work. But she was the most important one; the only person in a position to prove my innocence: Mr. Deal's very own personal assistant, Jakki, who had worked for him for twelve years. She spoke up against everything that her employer had fabricated. She supported my version of events. My lawyer said that in all her years of legal work, she had never seen anyone in Jakki's position take a stand like she did for me. Jakki was a ray of hope, the protection that came through from my Buddhist practice, in which I now immersed myself more than ever before.

In my local Buddhist group I made a close friend who became my own version of Keanu Reeves' 'Oracle' in the film *The Matrix*. Desperate to find his 'Oracle', Reeves searches high and low before eventually finding it in the guise of a homely black woman making tea in a high-rise apartment. Moriam was also a wise black woman and she lived on the top floor of a tower block just five minutes walk from my house. She was a source of never-ending spiritual support and encouragement. 'Come and chant with me today', she would insist. 'These problems of yours can kiss my black ass!'

I chanted to act with integrity, to drop my attachment to material things and to concentrate instead on developing self-respect. No matter how much injustice I felt, I had to take responsibility for having created this situation. It was my karma. And it had to change.

The day before the tribunal Steal and Deal backed down. We signed a compromise agreement and I was paid what I was owed in full. It was a victory of sorts, but at what cost? My mental health was in tatters.

I needed to get away. I needed to recuperate. So I decided to visit Louise and her daughter in LA. I carried a heavy weight, a failed career as I saw it, and of course, a broken heart. It felt so good to be in the endless Californian sunshine and soak up the laid-back atmosphere. We drove into the desert to spend time with her friends, Britt and John, in Palm Springs. We went hiking in the mountains, and rock climbing at Joshua Tree National Park. I scrambled to the top of the tallest rock and sat there, viewing the desert vastness from above. It was completely still, the silence broken only by the sound of rattlesnakes far below. At last I began to feel hopeful. Uplifted. At peace. I wanted to stay on that rock forever.

But it was straight back to reality when I flew home. Ten minutes after boarding who should walk into the cabin but Mr Deal. He took his seat right behind me and snored shamelessly for the entire flight back to London. Another sleepless night... *How much*, I wondered, *had I really changed?*

That desert rock high evaporated so quickly. Without a job, or even litigation to focus on, my love addiction now raged wilder than ever before. The news that Hermione had moved on to another relationship triggered what I can only describe as a trauma – a desperate petrified and endless fear that had me, quite literally, on my knees. As much as I knew I should let it go, I couldn't stop myself from contacting her. I would sob uncontrollably, begging her to see me. Sometimes I called her twenty times until she picked up the phone. Mostly she was able to withstand my pleas but on one occasion she came over. We started to argue and it escalated into a fight that ended with me pushing her hard across the room. Full of remorse, I hugged her close.

Please don't be broken. Please don't be hurt. I love you so much.

I was appalled at myself.

How could a Buddhist behave this way?

What was fucking wrong with me?!

I was no Treasure Tower. I was wretched. I was useless. I was no good for this world. I punched myself in the face, fist after fist, as if beating a drum of shame. Just for a moment the pain in my heart would ease, and then the dreadfulness would surge up and wash over me once again. I began to imagine jumping from a tower block, freefalling to my death and to the end of this pain. The Little Mermaid did that of course, jumping into the waves and onto her sword, turning the frothy sea red with blood.

Sometimes I curled up on the floor, sobbing in a heap for hours at a time. Once I heard the sound of a tortured animal and wondered where it was coming from. Then I realized that it was me. I was making that noise. Those screams and cries didn't even sound human.

Somehow I crawled to the place of my meditation and chanted the mantra. As I did, I prayed with all my heart, in such earnest desperation, the words in my head so clear. *Show me how! Show me how to have a healthy relationship!*

SHOW ME HOW!

And finally there was a shift. One day I found a shutter in my heart that separated me from my desperate emotions and I managed to pull it across. I stopped caring. About Hermione. About anyone. About anything. I went cold.

It was early November and my old school friends Wendy and Russell were having their fortieth birthday party. I drove up for the weekend, and hit the old school dance floor (with suitable drugs on board of course). Around midnight I took a few minutes away from the party and went upstairs for a break. As I walked into the office the music stopped me in my tracks. Of all the thousands of tunes that could have been playing from Russell's collection, it was a song featuring Hermione. Its haunting melody tried to seduce me, pulling me back into the nostalgic memories that I associated with it. I froze. It was just iTunes on shuffle but this felt way too close for comfort.

There was no way I was going back. If anything it spurred me on and I clutched even more firmly on that shutter in my heart. I picked up cocaine, caring nothing for those dead Columbian girls and nothing for myself. Later I went to bed with a guy I'd never met before and would never see again. We had numb, unsafe sex and didn't exchange numbers. I drove back to London alone. I was free. I was single. I could do what I wanted. I was a lone star. I had survived. I was moving on. The world was my oyster. Just keep my resolve, stay on my own, and I would be fine…

When the buzz wore off two days later, I crashed harder

and further than ever. Even Moriam couldn't console me. As I left her place after what had felt like a futile chant, I hesitated, feeling magnetically drawn to the edge of the balcony wall outside her flat. The movie in my mind was stuck on replay. Falling, falling, falling through the air to oblivion. Maybe it was time to do myself, and everyone else, a big favour. I stood by the balcony edge for some time, looking out across the view of London that I loved so much, only a few inches between my life and one final dive. *Not like this,* I thought. *This is not the way it ends.* I turned towards the elevators and took a slow walk home across the estate.

I stared at myself in the bathroom mirror. *Maybe an overdose. That would be easier.* Subtle. Less dramatic. Just go to sleep, sleep, sleep for a hundred years. I pulled out a bottle of Valium from the back of the cabinet. *Would this be enough?* Tired and frightened eyes looked back at me, set within a face that was thin and drawn. *Seriously*, I thought, *do I have another option?* My eyes were glassy. Blue. Like Nan's…

One last chant, I thought. *Let it be the decider.*

I sat down to chant, my mind open to a solution. It didn't take long.

Make the call, said the voice inside. *This is addiction and you know it. Make the call to someone who understands.*

I phoned Natasha. Dear, extraordinary Natasha. My friend of old. We didn't have much contact any more but I knew she had been to rehab and got clean.

She answered. I managed to get the words out. How I was feeling. How I wanted to die. It was time to give up. I couldn't do it any longer.

'Should I call Narcotics Anonymous?' I said.

'Yes', she said.

'I just want to find peace in my life.'

'Look forward to it', Natasha said with such surety that it struck me.

Look forward to it. As if this peace I longed for, that I had searched my whole life to find, was definitely there if I did this now.

A woman on the end of the NA helpline listened as I told her everything, how I hardly took drugs anymore, but when I did I blew out and then felt like dying. I told her about Hermione and the guy at the party and she said,

'Have you thought about going to SLAA?'

'No, what's that?'

'It's for sex and love addicts. It's a really strong fellowship and I think you might want to give them a call. They have a H.O.W. programme.'

Sex and love addiction? Really? I didn't even know that was a thing. Yet two weeks later I was going to these H.O.W. meetings that I never knew existed, for recovery from an addiction that I didn't even know I had.

Chapter Seven

Learning

Become the master of your mind, rather than let your mind master you.

Letter to the Brothers[1]

Learning to recover from addiction. Learning to heal.

For all that I had experienced before I went into recovery, the learning curve was about to get steeper than ever before. I needed Honesty, Open-mindedness and Willingness, the HOW of the H.O.W. programme.

Mind, body and spirit. In Eastern medicine they are viewed as the three legs of a stool; they require equal attention for maintaining strong and balanced health. In the West, extensive scientific research has also proved the power of our thoughts and emotions in healing the physical symptoms of disease. Learning to pay close attention to how we feel (our emotional or spiritual health) is the first step towards creating good mental health. In turn, good mental health promotes good physical health.

As I crawled into the Twelve Step recovery rooms at the end of 2006 I was in desperate need of all three. After five years of developing the spiritual aspect of my life I didn't doubt what my impassioned prayer *Show me HOW!* had generated in the physical world. A phone call to Narcotics Anonymous was the answer and I trusted it as fully as I trusted the knowledge that I now lay at the end of the shame-filled, heart-piercing, knee-breaking line.

Here it was. Absolute rock bottom.

The place to find absolute happiness.

It didn't feel like happiness of course. It felt terrifying. I railed against the idea of letting go and venturing still further into the unknown. But somehow I found a local meeting and plucked up the courage to go, chanting all the way as I drove there. What would I find in this relatively underground network of church basements and halls? Psychopaths? Rapists? My head was almost spinning with adrenaline by the time I reached the place – my heart racing. A friend recently told me that he went as far as taking his pulse during his first meeting. It was 180. Mine must have been something like it. I sat in the car trying to calm myself. Outside it was already dark. Eventually I saw people materialise out of the gloom, their faces eerily lit by the streetlights. I climbed tentatively out of the car and walked slowly towards the building entrance. Awkward, uncomfortable, self-conscious, embarrassed, stupid and ashamed.

Once inside what surprised me was how relaxed and normal it all felt. By the time I'd sat down at least three people had welcomed me as they light-heartedly carried on putting out chairs, arranging leaflets and making tea. When they realized I was a newcomer one particular woman was even friendlier, handing me her phone number in case I had questions once it was over. Candles were lit, and a peacefulness descended on the room as more people took their places. Maybe this was going to be OK after all…

It was during the meeting that, for the very first time, I learned the specifics of what sex and love addiction is. And as each characteristic was read out I found myself mentally ticking every box:

Becoming sexually involved with and/or emotionally attached to people without knowing them, with few healthy boundaries.

Well, yes. Wasn't that how you got to know someone in the first place?

Fearing abandonment and loneliness, so returning to painful, destructive relationships.

Here was the misery-go-round I couldn't get off.

Concealing our dependency needs from others, thus growing more isolated and alienated.

That was true too. Will. Hermione.

Compulsively pursuing one relationship after another, sometimes having more than one sexual or emotional liaison at a time.

I guess I'd already written a book on that one.

Confusing love with neediness, physical and sexual attraction, pity and/or the need to rescue or be rescued.

But wasn't that all part of being 'in love'?

The list went on, becoming more painfully accurate with each line.

Sexualizing stress, guilt, loneliness, anger, shame, fear and envy.

When didn't I feel like that?

Using sex and emotional involvement to manipulate and control others.

Guilty.

Becoming immobilized or seriously distracted by romantic obsessions and fantasies. Avoiding responsibility by attaching ourselves to people who are emotionally unavailable.

Here I stand.

Idolising and pursuing people then blaming them for not fulfilling our expectations.

Please, no more, I thought.

Then came the time for sharing.

Now more astonishment whipped up the air as I heard people speaking openly about their struggles in addictive relationships. Relationships that felt abusive or unconnected. Controlling partners or people who were never there. Obsessions and fantasies. Intrigue that lasted for years. Endless cyclical arguments. Lust. Infidelity. Anxiety. Sadness. Grief. Angst. It was all so familiar. As the meeting went on, I knew. Something that accounted for what had been 'wrong' with me for as long as I could remember.

I was stunned. How could I have sustained this for so long? At one level it was a relief to realize the accuracy of a diagnosis, but seriously…? A sex and love addict? *How was I going to explain this?* Alcoholic – possibly. Drug addict – for sure. Anorexic – maybe. Workaholic – I guess. But 'sex and love addict'? Try discussing that at a dinner party… If heroin were to have a perceived degree of *chic*, sex and love addiction was most definitely *freak*. Without the people in the fellowship there was no way I could have come to this understanding on my own.

The days that followed were a blur, as I made my way from one meeting to the next, my head spinning with information along with one dawning realization: life was never going to be the same. I was encouraged to stop all contact with Hermione and I knew in my heart that was right. I committed to not calling her whenever I was in pain, which amounted to the same thing as never contacting her – I was always in pain when I wanted to call her. And if I wasn't in pain, I didn't need to speak to her, revelling briefly in a sweet sanctuary of momentary calm.

One day I was almost manic in my desperation to pick up the phone. *Get to a meeting!* intuition told me. Frantically I searched the meetings list. There was one starting in the West End in an hour. I set off. A girl on a mission…

First I drove to the wrong Duke Street. *Who knew there were two?* But I refused to be defeated. I had to get there. It was the only place I would find relief from my crazy thoughts. I stop–started through slowly moving cars and taxis, desperate to reach the meeting before it began. Now, on foot. *Was I even walking in the right direction?* In the middle of Oxford Street on a Thursday night, packed with Christmas shoppers, trying to run against the intense throng, swerving between Selfridges' bags and happy couples making their festive purchases together, there I was, weaving my way through 'normal' life to seek emotional relief.

And there they were; waiting for me. My exquisite group of sex and love addicts in all their beauty, all their fragility, sitting there with their wounds, their scars, their stories like mine, their acceptance of this pain. They had already found the courage to face their truth, and now they offered a place for me. A chair in a room where I could start to heal. I let out a sigh of relief as I joined them in the serenity prayer:

Grant me the serenity to accept the things I cannot change, the courage to change the things I can, and the wisdom to know the difference.

There had to be a solution here. And it had to work.

Tears streamed down my face as I drove home later, one more time down the Marylebone Road for the ten thousandth time in my London life. They continued to flow for many days and nights to come on that familiar journey home. This was life now in early sobriety, feeling the emotions that I had avoided for so long, finally facing a truth that had been there since I was a child. This was nothing to do with the ex-girlfriend, the ex-boyfriend, this lover or that partner. This was all to do with *me*. I went *into* relationships broken-hearted. I had gone into my *teens* broken-hearted, I had gone through my *life* broken-hearted. I just was *broken-hearted*. Was it ever possible to recover and live a normal life?

I chanted to find a sponsor who would take me through the programme. And it was when I started to read out loud to her that the floodgates truly opened. As I shared my history I sobbed like a child. Distraught. And yet for all my fear that I would never be able to handle the painfulness of the truth, I found relief. It was all there within me anyway, affecting everything. Admitting it made it slightly better, not worse. Such is the act of 'surrender'.

Along with a programme of physical abstinence and withdrawal, all Twelve-Step fellowships encourage a practice of prayer and meditation while addressing the mental or cognitive aspect of addiction. When neurological pathways have been misaligned, or are painfully or destructively wired, they need re-wiring. Addiction is a psychological, as well as a biological and social disease. It has to be treated at every level. Mind, body and spirit.

After admitting a physical powerlessness over our addiction, we are invited to develop a connection with our 'higher power' or the 'god of our understanding'. We then learn to surrender our addiction to this higher power. Some people call their higher power 'God', which they might regard as a benevolent force outside of themselves. For me it was my Buddhahood – my inner being – the highest level of my consciousness – my higher self.

The first three years of sobriety were brutal.

It started off hard; a breathtaking withdrawal that was sometimes so painful I would fall to my knees. Bottom lines were my no-go behaviour, what defined my personal sobriety from sex and love addiction. No sexual contact. No romantic involvement. No fantasy. No cruising. No intrigue. No contact with the ex. All the things I had used compulsively as an escape or just to get high. At some point I would revisit them within a healthier context – but for now, celibacy.

For the first thirty days each day felt like a month. The dark, searing ache did not stop, not for a minute, even when I was chanting. It was all I could do to get through. I called my sponsor daily. I called other members of the fellowship too. And every day I did written work before reading it aloud. I also went to a meeting most days. There I found relief as I shared my struggle and listened to someone else's. My fellows encouraged me to keep going. They inspired me to stay focused on the goal of living a life free of addiction. One of my fellows said it was like a mountain to climb. But one day, they said, there would be a magnificent view. I dug in.

After fourteen days I got honest about my use of substances too. It was after a glass of champagne at a friend's fortieth birthday. Within an hour I was at sea, my emotions tossed around in a place that felt far from safe ground. Drink and drugs were on the path that took me away from the source of my serenity, not closer. I had used getting high to try to fix my broken heart and make me feel better about myself. Getting high, I now realized, was also part of what I mistook for intimacy. Not once in my life had I slept with someone for the first time without using alcohol and/or drugs. Never. Not once.

Right there, in the midst of this already excruciating withdrawal, I took an additional vow of sobriety. I joined Narcotics Anonymous to help me put down drink and drugs. A new wave of humility washed over me as I admitted my powerlessness once again. Unlike love addiction, which often starts in childhood, drug addiction usually develops during teenage years. It bears the hallmark of being out of control. *Fuck it. Who cares? What's the point?* Recovery from substance abuse is black and white. You put it down for good.

Ninety meetings for ninety days, they said. And that's how these early days of sobriety were for me. Cold turkey. No clinics. No rehab. No therapists. Just my fellows and me. And, in spite of all the highs and lows that had come before this, for all of the trauma, the escapism, and the extremes, the journey into sobriety became the ultimate white-knuckle ride.

I clung on for dear life. Now that I had stopped acting out, this dramatic ride was on the inside, just keeping those bottom lines. A trip to the petrol station, for example, appeared uneventful. Instead of scanning the forecourt for flirtatious looks from other drivers, I kept my eyes on the petrol meter, its flickering numbers winning my devoted attention. Then I glued my eyes firmly to the ground as I went to pay.

I changed the sound track to my life – literally. I ditched the doped-up, chilled-out, get-your-pants-off music that had permeated my relationships of recent years and returned to my indie roots, listening once more to creative lyrics and connecting with a long-lost part of myself. A Mos Def track touched the nerve of my revelation: *The riot is easy and the silence is loud. You can build yourself up by just turning things down.*[2]

When the urge to project myself into a fantasy world grew strong, I would talk myself out loud through the job in hand: 'I am standing at the ironing board right now and I am moving the iron one way and the next across my jeans, which are blue, and I am standing here right now, doing the ironing…' and so on, until the moment passed. How liberating to know that it was even possible. The programme called this retraining of the mind 'staying present'.

The Buddha's words resonated poignantly, taking on a

deeper meaning than ever before: *Become the master of your mind rather than let your mind master you.*[3]

This became my mantra, moment by moment, as I battled to let go of the urge to escape. So much of life had been spent either regretting the past or projecting my fears into the future. How little time I had spent in the here and now, either enjoying it or taking responsibility for it.

I drove to Yorkshire to spend Christmas with Nan. Just Nan and me. Not only was driving up the motorway a fantasy-free experience, once settled in I was present 100 percent, giving her my complete and heartfelt attention. When it was time for the daily sponsor call, I retreated to the bedroom while Nan watched Christmas TV, a thin wall of plaster separating an intense narrative of sex and love addiction from her vigilant ears. Not once disappearing into the fantasies in my head, or getting distracted by some relationship drama, I returned to that place of contentment I had known as a child as I sat peacefully in Nan's company over the holiday.

At the end of thirty days, not only had I made it through a month of sobriety, I had also completed the first three steps, adapting them comfortably, confidently and unapologetically to align with my Buddhist understanding. For me, there was never a conflict of ideas or principles, rather a natural fusion and application of the two working together. I even reworded the Twelve Steps slightly. Semantics, I know. But it felt right for me.

Step One. *Admit that we are powerless over addiction, that our lives have become unmanageable.* Summon up the courage to face reality; the first step of true surrender. And by admitting that I just couldn't help it, I found relief.

Step Two. *Believe that a power greater than ourselves will restore us to sanity.* My inner being or my greater self knows that addiction does not define me. Rather it knows me for the healthy, happy person that I truly am. Believe this.

Step Three. *Make a decision to turn our will and our lives over to the care of our higher power.* Here lies the basis of a spiritual recovery from addiction: the absolute necessity to connect with our greater self; a decision we take minute by minute as the process of letting go unfolds.

They were intense, those early days. Learning to make my way within this new community of addicts, all of us equal in our shared and common goal, no one responsible for anyone other than him or herself. A group of us bonded over dinner after the Saturday evening meeting and shared heartfelt conversation. It was fun to have dinner without bottles of wine on the table. It made for a richer quality of conversation. As we got to know each other better the level of humour rose. One evening in a bustling West End restaurant I was talking about how shy I had been in the playground as a child and how difficult it was to make friends. I related how my parents had tried to coach their little six-year-old. 'All you have to do', they had said, 'is go up to a group of children and say "My name is Ruth and…"' Before I could finish my sentence the group spontaneously all chipped in loudly together, *'I'm a sex and love addict!'* The startled diners looked around and we all laughed loudly. Shame was beginning to lift.

Step Four. *Make a searching and fearless inventory.* A close-up look at a previously addictive life through freshly sober eyes. All the resentments, the fears, the dishonesty and the harm I'd done to myself and to others. I identified every significant moment when I had failed to believe in my greater self (or theirs) and had searched instead for love and happiness in all the wrong places.

As I sat on my couch day after day, writing it down and feeling it fully for the first time, I started to gain perspective on how I'd acted out sexually, right from the beginning. How my sexuality was linked to a painful cycle of unworthiness, abuse, fear, rejection, conflict and hurt. In this process I could find myself sexually aroused, crying tears of regret and sadness, angry and ashamed of myself, sometimes all at the same time. It was an unpleasant and difficult process, yes – only to be done once before moving on, but it was important to acknowledge the exact nature of what I needed to change. I was building a new life from the foundations up.

Step Five. *Admit to another human being the exact nature of our addiction.* To make it real I read it out to my sponsor, a massive declaration of my regretful behaviour, my unmanageability, the dark places that addiction had taken me to. And, as my patient and generous sponsor accepted me, so I started to accept myself.

Steps Six and Seven were about the way it was now. A spiritual clean up. Step Six. *Be entirely ready to change, to expand and to grow.* I identified the aspects of my personality that had caused the greatest unhappiness in life. Arrogance, impatience, perfectionism, the way I judged others and myself, but most of all, a lack of faith in my higher self. This self-doubt would always be at the root of my unhappiness.

Step Seven. *Earnestly pray to raise and improve our life condition.* This was spiritual practice. Chanting to transform all of this poison into medicine. Now sober, free from addiction, I could allow genuine humility to emerge. I felt a noticeable shift in consciousness at this stage from *What can I get?* to *What can I give?* Now my focus turned to the person I wanted to be. To my true self.

In this moment of awakening I realized that this inner being was by far the greater part of me, my physical existence so transient and temporary in comparison. Instead of a human being trying to walk a spiritual path, I was actually a spiritual being trying to walk a human path. Things made more sense. Something about life's true purpose was starting to emerge.

And so, these first few months of sobriety were the beginnings of developing a truer relationship with myself, one based on honesty and authenticity. In the process I noticed how few boundaries I had. So much of my life up to that point had been 'fuck it' or 'anything goes'. Now I had to learn to set limits. What I could accept. What I could not. For myself and with others. So often I had done this the other way around, letting other people define their boundaries while I tried to fit in around them, bending myself out of shape, flexible to the point of spineless. Now I felt like a child learning how to do life, but this time in a functional way rather than as a survivor.

And then I learned about triggers.

Step Eight. *Make a list of people we have hurt and become willing to make amends to them all.* The step where we focus back into the world and clean up our relationships, amend the consequences of our past behaviour wherever possible, and then draw a line in the sand. It was a long and shameful list of lovers (and sometimes their partners), friends, family and work colleagues, all of whom had suffered from the blatant denial of my higher self and theirs. I'd hurt them, even if they were not aware of it, even during my Little Mermaid moments when I'd given my life away for the validation or the grandiosity of love.

Step Nine. *Make direct amends to such people wherever possible.*

And this was where the trouble started.

I lifted the embargo on contacting Hermione and we made a plan to meet. Immediately, I became anxious and agitated. *Would she still want me? Had she found someone else?* My still bubbling addiction had been triggered by the possibility of a potential buzz or more heartbreak.

It was a grey afternoon on Parliament Hill and the clouds hung ominously over the London skyline as we greeted each other for the first time in six months.

We walked side by side along the footpath. Mothers pushed babies in prams, kids rode their bikes, runners jogged past, and there we were, edging ourselves back into awkward conversation. I was there to make my amends, apologise for my part in the conflict and hurt between us. That wasn't so hard. I said what I needed to say. Hermione listened. She accepted my apology. No arguments. Peace.

It was where we would go from here that created tension. Hermione said she wanted us to be together and that she'd missed me. That she'd realized her mistakes too. I backed away. How could she be so sure when she didn't know the *real* me anymore? Didn't she want to see how much I had changed? I wasn't the same person I had been six months before. And was she even the right person for me?

We parted with a suggestion that we spend time getting to know each other again. But my sponsor, when she heard, said she saw my mind cloud over. It was true. Just seeing Hermione was confusing. I had lost clarity.

And then, almost simultaneously, there came a bolt from the blue.

Nan collapsed at home.

I took the call from my father on Good Friday as I sat down for dinner at a friend's house. She'd been admitted to Barnsley General with breathing difficulties. I drove up immediately. When I walked in I found her lying in an open ward, pale and fragile. She was happy to see me, and we chatted, but then a terrible cough erupted for several minutes, exhausting her. She needed to sleep. I left with an uncomfortable feeling, nervous about a trip to Mexico later that week, where I was supposed to be meeting Louise for her fortieth birthday.

Hermione was surprisingly unsympathetic. She said she was struggling about the trip to Mexico, even though these were plans I had made during our time apart. Our connection was growing increasingly uneasy and tense. Yet my dependency on her had already been re-activated and I started to twist myself in knots, trying to think of a way to soothe the rising conflict. With at least one foot back on that misery-go-round of old, my other foot may still have been on the ground, but I was hopping along madly as the ride was gaining momentum.

I went to Mexico regardless, meeting Louise, Britt and John on the idyllic beach of Tulum. It was another seaside paradise. But for the first time in my recovery to date, I struggled to remain present, torn between my thoughts of Nan in hospital and Hermione in London. Withdrawal was on me, harder than a hammer smashing glass. Isolated, I found myself calling Hermione from the beach. And there I was, back on the dreaded ride. Caught up in some compulsive, futile argument that just went round and round. I sank into such massive shame that I was numbed into silence – all clarity gone. I knew this couldn't be love.

Nan was still on an open ward when I got back. Her cough had deteriorated. She was tired and depressed. I could sense tension between Mum and Aunt Sue, both of whom had been by their mother's side constantly. Mum wanted Nan to stay in hospital, Sue wanted to take her back home. The medical staff were reluctant to intervene.

One look at Nan and I knew that she was in the last few days of her life. The hospital ward was not fit for purpose but there were no individual rooms available. Nan had no quiet and no privacy. I would have wanted to be at home if it were me, safe and comfortable in my own bed. Mum and Sue were bent over with exhaustion so I offered to stay on the ward for the night. Mum would drive back home and Sue stay at Nan's place nearby. After Nan settled to sleep, I was given a small camp bed in a storeroom. I chanted for as long as I could before the desperate need to sleep took over.

At around 2 a.m. a nurse slipped in to wake me. A single room had become free. Could I help move Nan into it? It only took five minutes but the difference was immeasurable. With relief, I pushed Nan's bed through the warm rays of light framing the doorway. It was like a parallel universe. Surely this was the perfect compromise to Mum and Sue's dilemma that I had prayed for.

By morning, however, Nan was distressed. She kept trying to lift herself out of bed, clutching at the sides of her bed in pain. Pain in her lungs. Pain from her incessant cough. Pain in her kidneys. We talked.

'I'm dying, aren't I?' she asked.

'Does it feel like it?' I said. Nan's face grew more pained,

'Yes. Please get me out of here.' I was quick to agree,

'But you have to tell me where you want to go.'

Nan looked out of the window and thought about it, gazing into the distance towards the green moors that stretched to the horizon. She didn't reply. She didn't know. I kept asking the nurses for stronger medication. Something to help Nan relax, to help with her pain, to help her sleep. They said that the results weren't back from the lab so they couldn't prescribe.

Aunt Sue and I did what we could that day, comforting Nan when the coughing fits came, talking to the staff constantly, asking for progress by the hour. Eventually the results came in, and then it was clear. Lung cancer. Finally, a syringe driver was released with sedatives, tranquilizers and morphine. Nan relaxed for the first time in three weeks and fell into a peaceful sleep. I stayed by her side, stroking her hands, her arms and her legs. Minutes became hours and now time really did stand still. Breathe in. Breathe out. *Nan I love you. I adore you. I owe you my life.* I felt so close to her. And I felt the cycle of life and death in my arms. As she had held me in the first few hours of my life, so I held her in the last few hours of hers. Breathe in. Breathe out… Eventually Aunt Sue took the night shift by Nan's side, and I went to sleep at Sara and Tony's house nearby, crashing into exhausted unconsciousness as my head hit the pillow.

The next morning the family imploded.

It was a gruesome finale that bordered on grief-stricken slapstick. A kind of macabre *Carry on Dying* without the slightest sense of irony. Everyone's source of unconditional love, our beloved matriarch, was leaving. The blast of family karma took me sideways.

My parents arrived at the hospital already upset with me. According to my father, Mum felt 'ganged up on'. Their deep resentment radiated towards me: not an unfamiliar energy – but on the day I was to lose my beloved grandmother, it cut deeper. I grieved threefold, for the loss of Nan, for the daughter I wanted to be to my mother, and for the father I had always wanted. Where was that strong man who just wanted to put an arm around his little girl and tell her that everything was going to be OK? And after all I had done in those past two days…

I now see that my mother was losing her mother. And she had to do it her way. She didn't need me there. I should have left. *Why didn't I?* Then my father threatened to leave, bullying me into going outside with him. I refused, scared of what might happen. I was frightened like the eight-year-old girl scared of the good hiding. So there we were, the three of us, arguing over my Nan's dying body. And as always, I was to blame.

My brother Mark arrived. Mum and Dad read from their prayer books as Nan declined. When they went downstairs for tea, I helped the nurse wash and straighten Nan out. She slipped into odd positions, so we made her comfortable again. Her organs were shutting down one by one, and her skin looked paler and more translucent with each passing breath. It was a peaceful moment, oddly, and I said a provisional goodbye, promising to hold her in my heart eternally until we were born together again. Maybe her spirit would become my own son or daughter one day. I wanted this so much, to give birth to the new life of my dearest grandmother. Unconditional love. Breathe in. Breathe out. Breathe in…

I realized that supplemental oxygen was the only thing keeping Nan alive. When the nurse said we should probably take it away and I agreed, my regret was instant. Nan became like a fish out of water, gasping for air, struggling and spluttering. I was horrified. *What had I done?* My parents came back into the room, then rushed to open their prayer books: *The Lord is my shepherd, he leads me to green pastures…*

I couldn't bear it. I went downstairs and sat on a bench outside. I made some calls. Then I saw Mark leaving. When I called him over, he tore into me. Mum didn't like me, he said. *He* didn't like me. He didn't like anything I stood for: my jobs, my life, the car I drove, everything. It felt like years of resentment pouring out of him, triggered by his grief. And then his phone rang and it was my father to say that Nan had passed. It was over.

I fell into Mark's arms and sobbed.

We went back up to the ward, and there she was, peaceful now. I could hardly look at my parents. Never had the gap between us felt so wide. I took the hug I needed from one of the nurses. Then I went back to Nan's place and slept on her sofa for the very last time.

Grief and withdrawal took over as the days and weeks passed. Step Nine felt too big for me. The relationship with my family seemed unbridgeable. At the funeral I sat with Aunt Sue and Uncle George, hardly speaking to my parents. We laid Nan to rest in the churchyard in Darton. I read something at the graveside, something my mother asked me to read. *What was it? What did I read that day?* My brother spoke at the wake, as he fought back tears, his voice shaking like a child's. But he did it. Unlike me. I stood mute, unable to voice a word. I didn't shed a tear all day, not because I wasn't feeling anything, but I knew that if I had let out even one drop, the floodgates would have burst. I would have thrown myself into the grave with Nan, so wretched was I.

At home I called Hermione. She pushed me away. My knees buckled. This was it. I was hitting the floor again. Another rock bottom…

But instead, something else happened. Something totally unforeseen.

Amazing grace.

Before my knees hit the floor I picked up the phone. And my sponsor was there. She reminded me of all the work I'd done to get to this point, of my journey, of my commitment to the truth, of my devotion to recovery. She guided me back onto the path and told me of the need to carry on. Just for today. One step at a time. And as we spoke I realized that to make my amends with other people, I had to first make amends with myself. I didn't have to do this all on my own. It was time for professional help.

I first met my addiction therapist on a sunny afternoon in August. Her office was in Duke Street, in the same building as those early recovery meetings. After telling her about my family fall-out, how I had vowed never to see my father again for the rest of my life, and how I had swerved way too close to the destructive relationship with Hermione in what should have been a process of making amends, she gave her opinion. She acknowledged that my work in the Twelve Step rooms had got me off the battlefield. Had I not already done this, she said, she would have recommended three months of residential treatment in a clinic. It started to dawn on me then, how broken I had been six months before as I'd limped my way between meetings and phone calls, clinging on for dear life.

I relaxed a bit, and asked her about my deepest fear. *How was it possible to get better from this? Wasn't I simply too broken?* She surprised me with insightful optimism. She cited the X-Men, the mutants with superpowers who were educated into becoming part of the human race to create peace, instead of destruction and exclusion from normal life. I liked this analogy. It resonated with the idea of transforming poison into medicine. Here was a mental health professional on a compatible philosophical line.

My very own Marvel Girl! I thought. She could be *Bright Lady!* Here was someone who had already harnessed her super powers – intellect, reason and empathy, possibly even telepathy – for the greater good. I wanted to do that too. We agreed to work together once a week and I would take outpatient treatment at a clinic later down the line.

On the subject of my family, this was Bright Lady's deal:

'You might not want to hear this right now, but my objective is for you to get to a place where you can happily be in the same room as your father, and even if he were to be at his very worst, you would be completely unaffected by it.'

'Actually, yes! That's exactly what I want!'

And so we began the long and meticulous process of working through each part of my life, my history, my family of origin, one week at a time, healing what needed to be healed as it came up. Understanding karma the way I did, I knew it was me who needed to change. I didn't want to despise my father or disregard my mother. I wanted everything to be different – but the change had to come from me.

I thought back to the Buddha's promise that faith in the *Lotus Sutra* will benefit not only ourselves but the seven preceding generations and the seven generations that followed.[4] If only I could apply this truth now, in this lifetime, I could change my entire family's karma. When I'd held Nan in those final hours, I felt the continuum. Our energetic connection was real. Our heart-to-heart bond transcended lifetimes.

Shortly after meeting Bright Lady, my mother gave me Nan's diamond engagement ring, left for me in the will. Then I knew that Nan had never lost hope in me. I had to win. For me. For her. For everyone.

Step Ten. *Continue to become happy – to change, expand and grow.*

Step Eleven. *Seek through prayer and meditation to improve our conscious contact with our inner being.*

Step Twelve. *Carry the message of recovery to those still suffering, and practise these principles in all our affairs.*

Together these three steps form the basis of functional living, day by day. They are a foundation for a clean and sober life: take responsibility for your personal growth, strengthen your relationship with your higher power, and share your recovery with people who seek it. Give service. Addict or no addict, it's no bad way to live.

As the weeks and months passed, the quality of my life improved. I was present, I took responsibility, I felt alive. Friendships, which had always been essential to my survival, took on a deeper significance. Now I could truly appreciate my friends and engage with them fully. This wasn't always easy, but it was much more rewarding than it ever had been. I felt less needy, less entitled, and more appreciative.

Having a place to stay in Derbyshire when my Nan passed away was like having a second home, an extended family. Sara was more than a friend, she was like a sister, having known me from when I was eighteen. Despite all my flaws she and Tony had even shared their children with me, my godchildren. They were also my family. I realized how fortunate I was to have kept anyone throughout my years of addiction, what with my self-absorption, my selfishness, my unavailability...

As I went into my third year of sobriety I appreciated all the other friendships I had managed to bring with me despite everything. Good friends from school days, from university, people I'd met through work, ex-partners like Paul C and Gina who had truly seen the very worst of me and still cared. Even friends from clubbing days, who lovingly stood by me no matter what, in particular my friend Steve, who took me with him to the Glastonbury music festival where he was working. Being sober in that particular case was a big asset; he knew I would behave responsibly in the serious production environment backstage. The experience was a gift. I was completely captivated by the Glastonbury festival, all the way from behind the Pyramid stage, right up to the Twelve Step tent in the Green Fields, where I would go to a meeting every day. Wherever I was, I felt supported. Safe.

In the fellowship I made several new friends, some who came, some who went. One was Mary, a yoga teacher, who invited me to her family home in Spain for holidays, offering yet another sanctuary of peace and warmth. On one of our visits Mary introduced me to a close friend of hers, a woman called Laiya with whom I also connected straight away.

Heartache and suffering had rippled through Laiya's life, including the all-too-recent trauma of her sister's suicide. She shared all of this with me, and I was able to embrace her fragility. Even Mary described us as 'kindred spirits'. One evening Laiya and I discovered that we shared the same birthday. We called each other 'sister twins' from then on and continued our friendship once we were both back in London. Like Mary, Laiya taught yoga. I trusted her open spirit and kind heart. Although busy with our respective lives we spoke regularly and I felt that Laiya and I had a deep understanding, a shared bond of trauma that we were trying to resolve through our persistent hope for a better tomorrow. Laiya felt more vulnerable than me somehow, maybe less clear about her spiritual path, and I wanted to share with her what I had discovered.

With the 'romance' aspect of addiction under control, it was now time to face the 'finance'. As much as I had used sex and love as my 'fix', money was a toxic catalyst. Financial imbalance was often part of the relationship cycle, and money frequently represented stress. My career had hit extreme highs and lows. There was always so much fear and anxiety as well as excitement and possibility.

Ten years before, I had come out of the Internet business with almost a million pounds of liquid assets. Now, when I totalled up my liabilities, I was almost as much in the red as I had once been in the black. My sponsor encouraged me to go to the fellowship for people with money issues, either through debt, overworking or underearning. It was time to take financial responsibility.

Sobriety meant living within my means, not taking on any more debt or accepting work that paid less than I needed. With no income, no savings, high living expenses and few prospects, this seemed impossible, but I was determined. I threw myself into the project with a vengeance, selling anything that was surplus to my basic needs while I looked for a regular job. I took stuff to cash converters, I sold clothes I didn't wear, I did cleaning jobs for a friend, I sold my bike, my second property, everything... Sometimes I would need fifty pounds in the morning to pay an outgoing bill so I would empty my wardrobe and head to the Notting Hill vintage stores – often paying in the cash one minute before the bank closed for business. My reward? Another day of financial sobriety.

The employment situation was tough. It was 2008 and the UK was in recession. Most companies had stopped recruiting. Weeks turned into months. My search for work was proving fruitless. I was running out of things to sell, and even with my reduced spending budget I couldn't go on like this indefinitely. *Was I even going to lose my home?* In desperation I drove to the Buddhist Centre at Taplow Court in Buckinghamshire to ask for guidance. Spiritually I was having a crisis. The advice I received was clear:

Make a determination that you will find a job and then think nothing more of it. Pray only for this: to expand your heart and then share your faith with more people than you think is possible.

Another surrender. To place my faith above all my material desires, trusting that my prayers would be answered and my needs would be met. Re-energized, I continued. I shared the guidance with some fellow Buddhists over dinner that weekend and one of them said:

> *Faith puts you out on a limb sometimes. It edges you further and further along that branch until you get to the point where there is nowhere left to go but to jump. And when you jump, to trust that rather than falling into the depths of hell you will be completed protected. It is a test of your faith.*

I knew what he meant: to believe completely in my higher power, and to trust that my prayers would be answered. So I chanted for hours every day and gave as much service as I could whilst taking action to find work. I encouraged my fellow members. I studied. I sponsored several people in the fellowship. I told everyone I met about my practice. I opened my heart.

Soon after, I met a recruiter who immediately seemed different. Halfway through our first meeting he surprised me when he said,

'You know what is special about you? You are like a good wine. You have improved with age rather than going bitter. So many people in this industry turn bitter, but you haven't.'

Within a fortnight he had placed me in one of the top five design agencies, even though there was still an official freeze on recruitment. In fact, by the time they made their offer, another agency had made a counter-offer and I had to choose between the two. At last, I was solvent. I promised myself never to take money for granted ever again.

I set off to work each day using public transport, squeezing in a 6 a.m. yoga practice on the way, before getting to my desk at 9. There I reported to departmental directors, took a freelance wage, was told what to do by virtually *every* person in the team, no matter how young they were or how little experience they had. And I was so happy. My day started earlier than ever, but there was a spring in my step as I joined the rush-hour throng and felt the morning squeeze on the Jubilee Line, transcending smells of hangovers, garlic and sweat. Then I would burst onto the pavement at London Bridge, intoxicated by the fresh smells of flowers, coffee and baking bread as I spun through Borough Market. And I shared my exhaustion at the end of day with my fellow commuters in a stale and humid tube carriage, and on the congested roads home.

I took my place in society as an ordinary human being, living within my means, without my means defining me.

Freedom.

I was learning.

I was learning to walk free.

Chapter Eight

Realization

It is rare to be born a human being. The number of those endowed with human life is as small as the amount of earth one can place on a fingernail. Life as a human being is hard to sustain – as hard as it is for the dew to remain on the grass. But it is better to live a single day with honour than to live to 120 and die in disgrace.

The Three Kinds of Treasure[1]

What would learning be without realization? The moment when thought becomes actualised, absorbed, incorporated, part of who we are.

Embodied.

It was a focus on my bodily functions that had originally taken me to Margie's colonic clinic, and it was the physical fallout from a night of sex and drugs that took me into recovery. Excess teenage drinking, starving myself as a student, extreme exercise in gyms, long drug-fuelled party nights that turned into mornings that turned again into nights, erratic eating patterns throughout, not to mention the physical effect of narcotics and smoking… By the time I hit emotional rock bottom, the years of excess were manifesting physically as chronic pain and digestive problems, both of which were depleting me.

I took the path of yoga for healing. If my spirit needed

Buddhism, and if my mind needed therapy, it was my body that needed yoga. We cannot *pray* ourselves fit any more than we can *think* ourselves healthy. It seemed obvious to me then. Now as time progresses and these three disciplines deepen, where one ends and the next one begins becomes less and less clear. They are mutually supportive and interlinked. Mind, body and spirit. As I am one, they are one.

I first connected with yoga at the end of 2005, just after the dismissal from my business. I met a yoga teacher on a Buddhist course and she invited me to join her on a teaching retreat in Egypt. For ten days I practised with her on a desolate beach on the Suez coast. The weather was pretty cold, the sea not at all inviting, and the small resort was remote. It was the yoga practice that captivated me. Each morning I reached up to the sky in a salute to the sun before diving down towards the mat, hands meeting floor before lifting myself up and then pressing down again. Working through the *asana* postures one by one I focused on the solid line of the horizon as I wobbled precariously on one leg, struggling to breathe deeply, searching for my connection with the hard, dry earth. Instead of finding escape in the sparkling blue water, now it was time to get grounded.

During the day we would climb the mountainous cliffs that backed onto the beach, then sit at the top, looking out across a shimmering sea and vast skies above. It was peaceful there. And beautiful. I liked this North African, Middle Eastern landscape that was so dry and barren and huge all at the same time, and that just felt so... ancient. On the way back through Cairo I visited the pyramids at Giza. The Great Pyramid of Khufu, the oldest of the Seven Wonders of the Ancient World, held me transfixed before the street hustle got too much. I retreated to the tranquil surroundings of the Mina House Hotel, from where I could take in the imposing views in peace. Special. Magical.

This trip to Egypt marked my first steps into the modern Astanga Yoga tradition. The Astanga School was founded in Mysore, Southern India, in the 1930s by K. Pattabhi Jois – 'Guruji' as his students affectionately called him. Astanga felt good for me from the start. The fixed sequence of postures, once learned, meant that I knew what was coming next and let me work at an increasingly deeper level. And it was dynamic, a set of continuous flowing movements with something called a 'vinyasa', a breath and movement, between each posture. I loved the fluidity of the practice and the fact that it was so energetic. It was challenging, requiring far more physical strength and flexibility than anything I had experienced in the gym. Yet I felt safe within its clear and logical structure. Back in London I carried on a daily practice, either at home or at the health club, replacing weight training and aerobics completely and finding everything I needed in this ninety-minute sequence. I could feel yoga supporting my health, and it naturally complemented my Buddhist practice, with its spiritual underpinning and its meditative rhythm.

To learn anything properly in life, one needs a teacher. Someone to set the bar, to show how it is done, to inspire. The student chooses their mentor because they recognise this, not because the teacher has set themselves up as a 'guru' who has to be followed. Good teachers transmit the original teaching, passing on what they have learnt and realized to their students. This is how a tradition is kept pure without mutating into a personality cult. Many Buddhist traditions hold the idea of the mentor–disciple at their heart. The same is true of Astanga. A great teacher shares selflessly with their students, who in turn devote themselves to mastering their practice and continuing the tradition. It is a constant process of education and communication, for teacher and student alike.

I had a lot to overcome in my teacher-student relationships, the scars of my abusive schoolteacher lying hidden beneath the surface for decades. Learning environments tended to stir up difficult and inappropriate feelings of shame. Margie's strict Buddhist guidance could often trigger feelings of self-doubt and unworthiness. Yoga too, with its central emphasis on the student-teacher relationship also revealed complex emotions. But I persevered. I sensed that it was crucial for my progress.

It was my first yoga teacher, Phil, who encouraged me to leave the gym and join a proper yoga studio. Unselfishly he directed me towards the source of the practice. Eventually I connected with a young and enthusiastic instructor called Joey and my practice began to progress rapidly. We went on retreats to Turkey where we stayed in yurts and practised for hours. I returned to being vegetarian and, as my old lifestyle slipped further into the past, my health improved. The breathing, the sweating, the stretching, the building of an internal strength, and the purification of the vital organs – yoga helped detoxify both body and mind. In my sobriety, I loved the natural release of endorphins, which gave a clean high without the depressing come-down afterwards.

Joey had been directly authorised to teach by K. Pattabhi Jois himself and we were away on one of Joey's retreats when we heard that his master had died in India aged ninety-three. We practised 108 sun salutations to mark Guruji's passing. Shortly afterwards when Joey announced that he was moving away from London I could feel a sense of panic and loss. I had become attached to him as a teacher. A good lesson to learn – be attached to the teaching not to the teacher! Part of my confusion, I also realized, was rooted in an intention to practice in India with Guruji himself. Now that he had passed away I felt less clear about my direction. I should not have worried. Just as the doors to Mysore seemed to close, new doors unexpectedly opened.

If yoga had been inspired by the masculine until this point, it was the feminine that would now take the lead. My new teacher arrived in female form, an extraordinary woman called Eileen who brought such profound depth and intensity to her work I was nothing short of intimidated. She shone such a bright light on my weaknesses that I was almost moved to give up. Who was I to practise in front of such brilliance? Yes, self-doubt was clearly at large. Yet I knew that Eileen had so much to teach me, and I was encouraged to continue by a fellow student who practised alongside me. Oz.

I had found the yoga community to be a little standoffish at times, but Oz was different. She was open and friendly, and we would shower and chat about our day's practice before going off to work. One day she came into the studio after some time away looking more radiant than ever. She was deeply suntanned, her face was shining, and her practice had progressed beautifully. As we caught up she was eager to tell me about a place in the south of India called Kovalam and an Italian teacher called Lino Miele who ran workshops there during the winter. 'I want to come next time', I said immediately, to which she replied, 'You should.' Shortly afterwards Oz left the studio to teach somewhere else and she parted without leaving her contact details. But somehow I had a feeling, a deep knowing, that I would be going to India.

After a few months working at the design agency near London Bridge I was ready to take a break. My thoughts returned to the place that Oz had told me about. *I need to get in touch with her*, I thought. *How can I do that?* Then, amazingly, the very next day, not more than two minutes away from my office, I walked straight into her in the local sandwich shop! After excited exclamations and cheerful hellos it transpired that she taught yoga just around the corner. Our lives had moved in the same direction. I told Oz how much I wanted to go to India. She handed me her email address. And so it was that I found myself on a plane that Christmas, destination Kovalam, a small fishing village on the Keralan coast, to practise with Lino, one of Guruji's most senior teachers. The trip marked three years clean.

The air was thick like a steam room as I stepped off the plane at Trivandrum, India's southernmost city. I had stubbed my toe just before leaving home and now, almost twenty-four hours and over five thousand miles later, it was throbbing painfully. As the climate consumed me, so did the atmosphere. The cab from the airport hooted its horn for the entire journey to the beach. Then there was a walk to the hotel in the blazing sun through tiny passageways and footpaths, escorted by a horde of Indian men, all shouting to each other as they carried my bags on their heads.

The hotel was set back from the beach and located right next to the yoga school or *yogashala*. A young Indian man in Reception welcomed me and asked for my passport. I refused to give it to him, which made him laugh. Eventually, after the details had been dutifully written down, I was shown to my room. With a huge sigh of relief I collapsed on the bed. I had arrived.

I pulled off my shoes and socks, my purple toe gasping for air. Wow, I really had banged it hard. Then I made my way to the balcony and took in the scene. There were palm trees all around and you could hear the sea crashing on the nearby shore. The setting sun exploded in deep reds and pinks. The sound of drums mixed with the smell of smoke fires. A light, warm breeze ruffled a string of colourful lanterns draped between the trees in the hotel garden. All my senses were alight. It was enchanting. I felt my heartstrings pull. *How I longed for a companion to share this.*

The following morning I woke early and made my way across the garden in the half light. The sound of the temple music stirred gently through the open corridors. In this moment an overwhelming sense of wellbeing and comfort rushed over me, and very strongly the thought arose that this was a place where I might want to die. What a curious thought, I registered in my heightened awareness. *I could die here...*

The *yogashala* was at the top of a long flight of stairs on a canopied rooftop. It was a place of such intensity, such controlled movement, with dozens of deeply breathing, energetically moving students, their mats packed closely together, and Lino moving between them, giving adjustments, supported by a few almost mythical looking assistants who seemed to glide rather than walk between the bodies.

Tentatively I took my place and started to move through the sequence, acutely aware of every thought, every muscle, every point of weakness, my limitations, my stiffness, my awkwardness, until gradually I began to move more freely and less self-consciously. And with this my body took its place alongside this energetic tribe of fellow practitioners and I embraced the continuing process of learning and realization that is fundamental to the yoga tradition.

It's all in your mind, Lino says.

Stretch your mind.

He is right. If Buddhism creates a transformation of the spirit, Astanga Yoga is its physical counterpart, both aligned with developing a higher level of consciousness. Even now when I am on my mat my thoughts, if untamed, can fluctuate between feeling either completely useless or somehow superior. Both views come from a deluded self, and neither is the truth. I practised once again to become the master of my mind and not let my mind master me. There is no destination. It is all a journey. And so it was.

In the weeks leading up to the trip, I had spent time studying a letter of encouragement from the thirteenth-century Japanese sage Nichiren to one of his female followers. In it he describes how the practice of Buddhism is like repeatedly dying something blue from the dye of the indigo plant, so that eventually one's faith becomes an 'even deeper blue' than the plant itself. Nichiren urges this woman in the wake of her husband's passing, to deepen her faith, to believe in her Buddha nature, and to trust her inner strength.

Women regard their husband as their soul. Without their husband, they lack a soul. Nowadays, even married women find it difficult to get along in the world. Though you have lost your soul, you lead your life more courageously than those who have one. Furthermore, because you maintain your faith in the gods and you revere the Buddha, you are indeed a woman who surpasses others.[2]

A chord had twanged pitifully within me as I read it, a sadness for having failed to forge a successful partnership in life. I too felt bereft. The more that I chanted about it, the more I realized that to transform my love life, I had to love my life. As it was. As I was. I had shared my realization in a Twelve Step meeting at the time: *To have a love life, I have to love life!* It was simple really. Happiness lies within. Love. Life. Love yourself.

Now here I was at Lighthouse Beach, and suddenly this young man who had greeted me on arrival a few days before, the young man to whom I had refused to give my passport, started talking to me about his life. His arranged marriage had failed, he said, but they had a small baby. He felt trapped, often depressed, sometimes suicidal. I explained my faith. How it was possible to change everything and become happy. That nothing was impossible. We just had to believe. Then he told me that his name, in Hindu, meant 'Life.' I laughed at the serendipity. And in my precious naivety I took my first step towards intimacy when 'Life' kissed me on Christmas Day and told me I was beautiful.

It seemed so natural to accept what the Universe had brought to me in the shape of this sweet young man, to accept this delicate moment, a first kiss that felt so tender and precious, so shy and innocent. I had yearned for it, yes. A longing that had pulled so poignantly at my heart as I'd stood on the balcony, the day of my arrival. But it was an important first step, beautiful and pure in the moment, and I bravely and hopefully took it. I trusted this manifestation of 'Life'. It felt safe to do so, and I put my faith more firmly than ever in my higher power. It was new and it felt good.

As the days passed, we started to need each other, and very quickly a shared anxiety of being apart crept up on us. He talked of leaving India and working in Europe. He said it would take him five years. I said it couldn't work, that the gap between us was too wide. I knew this logically, but in my heart there was a question mark. *But what if...?*

On New Year's Eve I was invited to a party on the roof of a place called Paradesh, a small guesthouse that sat at the top of the hill with panoramic views of the lighthouse, the bay and the trees far below. From the deck, with Oz and her friends, I watched an almost pyrotechnic sunset fade into a smooth crimson sea and a full moon rise from behind the trees to cast its light on our party. I felt on top of the world, and I realized that I had reached a place on the path of recovery that felt like some kind of summit. A peak that I'd trusted to exist when I first started out in those early days, just trying to get from one foothold to the next, all in the faith that some day I would appreciate a view from the top. Here it was, three years later. A view that was a million times better than anything I could ever have imagined. A feeling of such complete serenity and oneness. In this moment I loved my life for everything that it was.

I went back to the UK refreshed and optimistic. But I missed 'Life.' That particular aliveness I had felt with him was absent now. Being with someone, sharing secrets, private time, intimacy and a special friendship. I struggled to get on top of the longing.

On the work front things were going well. I accepted a permanent position reporting to the CEO, and settled back into my routine of early-morning yoga before jumping on the Jubilee Line from Baker Street to London Bridge. Sometimes, as I came down the escalator into the crowds of commuters,

I would imagine seeing 'Life' in the crowd, looking up at me, beaming his bright, warm smile. Like that moment at the end of *Slumdog Millionaire* when they find each other at the train station. There he was. He had come. He had found me...

I have now come to know that whenever there is a period of calm or a sense of achievement, the next lesson is close at hand. My Buddhist friend Rose likens this to the way bamboo grows, gnarling around itself slowly for some time to create enough strength to shoot up high. If my time in India had been a growth phase, it was now time for a gnarly patch.

One morning in the yoga studio a trainee assistant adjusted me in a particular posture without giving the right support. Eileen, my teacher, was already shouting over to her, '*No. No, you must support her spine!*' But it was too late. I showered in sickening pain, and by the time I made it to the office I knew I was in deep trouble. As I lay in bed later that night, I couldn't find one comfortable position, and the next morning I woke up with a terrifying, nauseous spasm. I'd known back pain before. This time it was off the scale.

I had three 'slipped' discs in my lower back.

Hardly able to put one foot in front of the other there followed weeks of icepacks, painkillers, physiotherapy, even hot water bottles down the back of my jeans between home and work. Once I stood on a busy tube platform frozen in pain, not knowing how I was going to make it up three escalators and two flights of stairs to get to the office. I couldn't bend over for a month, not even to put on my knickers. Sometimes I had to crawl along the landing just to get to the bathroom. I would break down and cry. I hated the assistant who had done this. I hated myself for letting it happen. I hated myself for feeling so weak. And I hated being alone. In the absence of physical strength deep self-loathing was quick to surface.

I put on weight. My body started to change shape. I grew a tummy. My joints stiffened. I lost my tone and gracefulness.

Internally, the suffering was even greater. I realized the attachment I had to my physicality and how I'd relied on it to carry me through. My looks, my strength, my flexibility, my height, my athleticism. It had all been a cover for the deep sense of powerlessness I'd felt as a child. I remembered how I would fantasise that I was the bionic woman, waking from dreams so real that I would search my pre-pubescent body for the surgical incisions the scientists had made while building me! Later, in my teens, I invested heavily in my physique. During the diving years the boys had even nicknamed me 'the body'. Now what had once defined me was slipping away. Without my physicality, who was I? My aloneness, my singleness, felt like harsh failure as I struggled to look after myself, uncomfortable in front of the TV with nobody to talk to.

But there was healing too. One bank holiday weekend I called my father in desperation and anger. Straight away he came, along with Mum, to offer support. They worked all day on my garden and then stayed to watch TV with me in the evening. I spent endless time with osteopaths and physiotherapists, working at tiny little exercises to strengthen my core. And I walked for miles. Through parks, along the Thames, everywhere. And as I did I realized that my love for life had to extend beyond my body and its limitations. I must accept and love myself whatever shape I was in. And if that meant being the happiest, most maternal figure that ever lived, so be it!

I started to use affirmations, suggested by Louise Hay in her book *You Can Heal Your Life*. Her studies revealed how deep thought processes directly relate to various health conditions and need to be reversed so that healing can take place. For my particular condition, for the affected vertebrae, her suggested affirmation was: *I love me.*[3] As I drove around town I would often keep this affirmation in mind, trying to change the deep-seated belief of not being good enough or worthy enough for love. On a stretch of road that I used frequently, one building became the focus of my attention as I kept the words *I love me* going though my mind. Imagine my surprise when one morning, in preparation for the Notting Hill Carnival, two guys were up on ladders painting the words I LOVE ME high up on the side of that very same building!

Once again I chanted to realize the treasures of the heart.

More valuable than the treasures of the storehouse are the treasures of the body. But the treasures of the heart are the most valuable of all.[4]

The treasures of the heart: love, acceptance and compassion. And with that prayer, with that letting go, I got out of bed one day and went back to the yoga studio. The pain had receded. I was mending. What had been a set-back had prompted such deep introspection that in the process I lost some attachment, and in its place transformed perfectionism into compassion.

That summer my friend Steve was working at the Glastonbury Festival again and for the second year invited me to join him. At first I didn't think I could meet the physical demands of camping at Glastonbury, even with backstage prerogatives like hot showers and catering. But by the time the weekend came around, I was in good enough shape to take a chance. I loved living behind the Pyramid stage. It was like all my teenage fantasies rolled into one, sharing space with some of the world's greatest musicians as they ate, hung out and warmed up for their performances, then revelling in the wings as they gave it their all.

One of the first things I did when I got there was walk up the hill to the Twelve Step tent, an essential grounding for me in the crazy, amazing festival atmosphere. At the end of the meeting, a guy came over to chat and we walked back to the main area. Conversation was easy and fun. We could swap injury stories, he having recently recovered from a road traffic accident. He asked me to see Snoop Dog with him the following day and as I walked away I thought, maybe just maybe I might have a Glastonbury date…

The next day, during the gig, Twelve Step Guy kissed me, and we instantly turned into a Glastonbury couple, planning our next event and hanging out together like we had known each other for years. Later that night we made out under a huge full moon, watching XX play at the Park Stage. It felt like the quintessential reward for all those months of struggle. The sun shone brightly all weekend and we ran around like teenagers, lapping up the best musical festival in the world, even making out in his tent one afternoon. A soul mate had appeared to share my journey

Back in London Twelve Step Guy made signs that he wanted to carry on. Was this Glastonbury fantasy turning into something real? For a second it looked like it could have been, but he vapourised fast, like a genie from the lamp out of which he had so mysteriously appeared. In therapeutic terms this is often explained as 'avoidance', whilst I 'addictively' reached to him to fix my insecurity. In more compassionate terms I now think of it as *neither of us being ready*. Either way, it was a hard realization, almost too hard to bear.

I fell headlong into a spiral of confusion and loss and shame. Now, as I walked through the park, I thought only of what a drain I was on the planet. How my life was worth nothing. I hung my head, unable to look anyone in the eye, guilty even for the air I breathed. *Who was I to take up valuable oxygen that could be used by someone else?* Bright Lady suggested that I go to the Priory Hospital for trauma treatment and their psychiatrist admitted me to the programme as clinically depressed. Meanwhile, with shocking – or maybe fortuitous – timing my employer announced a wholesale restructure of the business and I was made redundant. I left the office after my last day of work on a Friday evening and checked into the Priory the following Monday morning. It was that straightforward.

The Priory applied the therapeutic model developed by Pia Melody at her treatment centre in Arizona called The Meadows. Over there the programme was called 'Survivors' because it is aimed to help survivors of childhood trauma. Here it didn't have a name other than, quite unimaginatively, 'Trauma Week'. I realized a lot about myself during the five days of Trauma Week. How I had gone through various stages of 'adaptation' during my childhood. How my neediness sprang from feeling abandoned as a baby and being manipulated by my schoolteacher during that horrific grooming process. How heroic perfectionism sustained an illusion that being 'good' would enable me to escape my teacher's abuse and my father's discipline. How as a teenage scapegoat I'd deployed anger and rebelliousness to 'act out' my inner confusion. Each stage came with its own set of addictions.

I also learned about 'carried' feelings, 'real' feelings and how to distinguish between the two. How 'carried' feelings are those we take on from the adults around us while we are children, whereas 'real' feelings are our own. At one point during the week we did a role-play in which we 'gave back' the carried feelings to the people who had foisted them on us. The catharsis was potent.

I say 'we' because I shared the week with three other people who felt as desperate and broken as I did. We held ourselves together in the light of each other's vulnerability. We witnessed each other's stories. We helped each other connect with our 'inner children', still there, as part of our psyche, crying out for what they hadn't received back then. We started to learn how to love these 'wounded' parts of ourselves from our adult heart… the people we had become. This technique of self-parenting helped me learn to take the responsibility for loving my life. Leaving all blame behind and focusing purely on what can be done right now, self-parenting says, by its very nature, *I can love the wounded parts of me, because no one else is able to do it for me.*

I came to my personal work with trepidation. I was shocked by what was revealed. As the therapist took me back to the memory of a 'good hiding', she catapaulted me into the most frightening trauma. My heart raced as I relived the moment. I connected with a memory so deeply buried that when I hit it I found white-hot rage that ignited a deafening buzzing. I started to black out. It was terrifying. With my fellows urging me on I found the courage to go back there once more – taking those feelings that had never been mine, and giving them back to their rightful owner.

I came away from the hospital not sure if it had even helped. I felt so raw. So vulnerable. How could this really change anything? The advice was to rest, as if you'd had surgery. There was an open wound that needed to heal. It was a few days later that I realized the difference. How I had changed something. The realization washed over me during a job interview. Something in the way I spoke, the way I responded to the questions, the ease with which I held myself. And I wasn't depressed any more. I felt lighter. Stronger. Clearer. Something was coming together. I was calmer too. Not anxious. With money in the bank and my career on track I had confidence that a new job was just around the corner.

Practise, practise, then all is coming, Guruji would say to his students. I turned back to yoga with fresh determination and booked a flight to India.

Returning to Kovalam felt like coming home. I ended the year just as I had welcomed it on that special rooftop in that special place, and staying in the perfect room, overlooking swaying palm trees and flaming sunsets. The enchanting lanterns still hung in the trees, the black crows still squawked from dawn, the temple still played out a resonant 'Om' every morning. Familiarity was affirmed. Deeper. More comforting. And yes, of course 'Life' was there. I went with no expectations, knowing that our worlds were too far apart for us to be anything more than friends. Yet still he declared his undying love. He now had a new job in Bangalore, he told me, a few hundred miles away, and he was ready to leave his family, divorce, and get a job in Europe. I was all he wanted. We could be together. If only I would believe…

I considered this as I chanted each morning before daybreak, then laid my mat in the *yogashala* and practised to take steady breath through the postures. The energy of the *shala* and the yogis surrounding me intensified. My physicality returned and my practice deepened more than ever. But there was a sticking point – and it felt insurmountable. I had never been able to drop into a back bend from a standing position, and now in the light of my injury, it looked as though this would never be resolved. Lino said it was all in my mind, and I cried tears of frustration and self-pity as I absorbed the painful emotions that came up for me with this posture. Back bends are heart openers. They open the heart chakra and require the letting go of fear. I had never been able to do this fully, either physically or emotionally. The drop-back reflected so clearly, through my body, what was in my soul.

I thought about my heart. And about my unconventional life. I acknowledged my connection with 'Life'. The way I felt when I was with him. His warmth, his gentleness and intelligence. The computer industry was booming in India, like it had in the UK in the '90s. I had no doubt of his potential to make it. When all was said and done, what did I have to lose? Maybe it was right to find the courage to open my heart? Wasn't 'Life' a manifestation of my practice and of my faith? So I agreed to join him, to believe in his vision for a future life together in Europe. For now I would see him in India as much as possible, and we would have Skype for the weeks in between.

Soon afterwards 'Life' left Trivandrum for his new job in Bangalore, allowing me to focus on yoga and on forging deeper friendships with my fellow practitioners. Oz was there, shining brightly as ever. Once more she organised a party on

New Year's Eve, this time in honour of her friend Mandy from Australia. I loved this group of friends who met every year to share their practice and their lives. It felt good to be part of it. It felt like my tribe now.

Time flew, and my health improved as I sweated out each ache and pain and ounce of stress. On my way back to London I met 'Life' in Bangalore and we spent two days excitedly exploring the city. We ran up the main street, the MG Road, hand in hand, and walked arm in arm around the park at dusk. We talked about the future, about the life we would eventually have in Europe, about our hopes and our dreams. Then I flew home, committing to our long-distance relationship until we could be in the same country. After a few days I found work with a TV company in London. 'Life' called me every single day. Ninety days later I flew back there to be with him.

Now I was in love. With 'Life'. With India. With life.

We had little money but we didn't need it. It was enough just being together. We rode on his motorbike through crazy traffic. We sat and drank lassi by the roadside. We strolled through the botanical gardens at night. We watched India win the cricket World Cup on TV, and laughed at the fireworks and shouts of celebration coming from every house and apartment around us. While 'Life' was at the office I swam in a pool I'd discovered across the street from where we were staying. In the evenings I made supper. We watched *Om Shanti Om* and danced around the living room like Shah Ruk Khan and Deepika Padukone.

Back in London, we Skyped every day. He soon changed jobs again, having received an even bigger promotion, with a company boasting a major presence in Europe and with the promise of huge projects to work on. Our vision was coming together, and when I visited again we discussed next steps. But there was one thing that bothered me. Him and his wife still hadn't mentioned divorce to their respective families. He said he would do it but I wasn't convinced, and sure enough when he went home to break the news, he took one look at his three-year-old girl and couldn't bear to separate from her.

He was right about that, I know. But he wanted us to continue as before, with his family situation left unresolved, and I couldn't do that. It wasn't respectful. It would cause resentment. I needed commitment. Partnership. A family of my own. We were at an impasse. So we gave it all up for the sake of his family. It was the right thing to do. I had known the risk. It was a complicated situation, miles away, continents away, cultures away. But we both felt the heartbreak and it hurt like hell. As my dream for a life with 'Life' fell away I sobbed like a child, that all too familiar feeling of broken heartedness consuming me.

No way! I implored to my higher power in desperation.

I refuse to believe this is my destiny! I demand my true love now!

It was a delusion of course, thinking that my happiness depended on someone else. In my impassioned plea to the Universe I made a conditional demand, this time not to show me *HOW* but to show me *WHO*. For the first time ever I posted a profile on a dating website. But it was an action taken from a place of disappointment and heartache. We attract not what we want, but *what we are*.

It came of course. Almost immediately. A polite and gentle email from an Indian man who lived in London, three miles from me. His family owned a large company in India. He had an eighteen-year-old daughter and had been through a similar dilemma to 'Life' thirteen years before. He understood, he said, because he was at the other end of it and finally free of his long-failed marriage. He wrote long letters about it all before we eventually met. I was so moved by this, that the Universe had brought someone who deeply understood my recent heartbreak, and I trusted it, even though this man was very different from anyone I had known before. He came across as quite timid and shy and had an issue with one of his legs that made him limp. He had experienced trauma. But he showed strength in other ways. He was intelligent and thoughtful, and had clearly spent a lot of time in deep contemplation of life. He was passionate about the things he loved such as his electronics business and horse racing.

On our first date he said that I was everything he wanted, and that until I told him to go away, he was devoted. It was music to my ears… His family owned several aircraft and he offered to fly me from Bangalore to Trivandrum later in the year. That sounded pretty cool too. For this, my friends at work called him Jetman. Jet Man. Had he finally arrived? My knight in shining armour? The man I had always waited for? I didn't know for sure, but I did have a sense that everything was going to be OK now that my prayer of WHO had been answered.

My friend Laiya squinted her eyes a little when I told her about my new beau. We'd met for afternoon tea after she'd taught her yoga class. I was impressed to observe her at work as she chatted with the receptionists and bounced happily around. Over tea however she didn't seem happy, and I thought that her skipping around at work had been more of an effort than I first realized. We walked down the King's Road, pleased to be catching some time together. I was excited to tell her my news. Yet she didn't look altogether pleased. *Maybe she feels left out*, I thought. *Or maybe she's concerned for me*. In any event I said that she and Mary should meet him.

'Lets all have dinner', I said.

'I'd like that', Laiya said.

And then, in the midst of everything, my dear friend Gina fell seriously ill. After suffering with a swollen stomach for some time she was taken into hospital where tests revealed advanced ovarian cancer. She started intense chemotherapy straight away, and I parted for India torn and concerned, not even knowing if I should be leaving London at all. She insisted of course, urging me to follow my heart's desire, wishing me nothing but the best, as true friends do.

The truth is that we accept the love that we think we deserve. I *wanted* to deserve the best and by the time I arrived in Kovalam with Jetman next to me, excitedly taking in a very 'private' view of the lighthouse as we flew in above the beach, I wanted to believe that I had found it. Although my heart still ached for 'Life', I pushed the feelings off to the perimeter, focusing on the companion who was by my side. This kind and generous man was so clearly the answer to my prayers.

Jetman checked into a five-star hotel nearby while I stayed at my usual place next to the *yogashala*. After two months of dating we hadn't slept together – first, because I hadn't felt the chemistry, and second, because this time I wanted to be sure. While Jetman fell asleep under fine cotton sheets, I saw 'Life' for the first time since our break-up and told him there was someone else. He sobbed like a child. I couldn't have said what I did without Jetman in the background. My feelings still ran deep.

Jetman wasn't an obvious choice for me. He was from a different world. Quite formal, very courteous, a little uptight. But he seemed to offer the stability that I had longed for. And he needed me in a way that I had never felt anyone need me before. As he began to open up and relax, his sense of humour came through. Sitting by the pool at his hotel room one day, I realized I could fall in love with him. I saw his essence, the beauty of his soul. From that moment I didn't look back as we plunged headlong into a fairytale romance. He pledged lifelong commitment as he flew back to his hometown for business, and I floated on a cloud, finally having met an intellectual equal who offered the emotional sanctuary I craved.

A few days later life changed for everyone in Kovalam.

Lino's school is a close community of practitioners, mostly teachers, who return year after year to share an intensive immersion in their practice. Oz had been a devoted student for many years, as were her friends with whom I was gently establishing my own connection.

We had been there a couple of weeks when Mandy arrived from Australia. She came early one morning and knocked excitedly on Oz's bedroom door. Oz, who hadn't been feeling well, answered, shared the animated reunion with one of her closest friends, and then turned to get back into bed. But as she did, she fainted, probably from getting up so fast, and her head hit the floor. The impact was enough to fracture her skull, and the internal bleeding sent her into a deep coma before she even reached the hospital. 'I'm OK' were her very last words before she descended into the deepest sleep.

After four days, still in coma, Oz passed away. She was thirty-four.

In this same place where I had arrived two years before, where I had felt such peace that I could die here, Oz actually had. So young. So beautiful. Yet she was called away suddenly, without warning or time to say goodbye.

We held a small ceremony on the roof of the Paradesh under a spectacular sunset of the deepest colours. We were invited to share our memories of Oz's qualities, so that they would continue with her into her next life. I heard 'emotional maturity', 'beauty', 'love', 'compassion', 'happiness', 'loyalty', 'generosity'.

Tongue-tied, I could not speak. There were no words. I could only look at Oz's dear friend Robin and shake my head in disbelief.

'She slipped off the edge', he said.

That was it.

She had slipped off the edge.

Practising in the shala while Oz was still in a coma had been emotional, her T-shirt hanging at the front, next to a photograph of Guruji. We had taken breaths for her, praying for a miracle, praying that she would make it.

On the morning that she passed away, one of Lino's assistants, Randa noticed that instead of the usual bugs and moths flitting around the solitary light bulb, there was just one single beautiful butterfly dancing and fluttering through the room. As I practised that day I could feel Oz's presence. Every breath and every movement felt more meaningful, as if the stakes in life had risen somehow. I felt a higher level of consciousness. I could feel things more deeply.

When it came to the backbends at the end of the sequence, I took my stand as usual, waiting for Lino to support me. But that day I heard a voice from within.

Do it! the voice said.

Do it on your own. You can do it!

It sounded like an Oz voice to me, cheerfully optimistic, and warmly encouraging.

Really? I thought. *Can I?*

Of course you can! Just do it!

And so, with a deep breath, I bent backwards on my own, reaching for the floor, until plop! I landed in a perfect arch; the wheel, the upward bow, *dhanurasana*, for the very first time.

So many deep realizations emerged in the days after her passing. Oz was a great teacher, in death as in life. In helping to open my heart, Oz enabled me to trust; she helped me believe in myself. She taught how precious life is, how fragile, and how we should cherish each day because we just don't know when the last day might be.

Oz taught us how to live and she taught us how to die.

Realization. In this moment I vowed not to waste one more minute of my life. To stay true to my ideals. To live only for today. And to live for love.

Here was Jetman, promising me the world, his love, his commitment, everything. I turned to face him and fully accepted his proposal to make a life together.

I still had so much to learn.

Chapter Nine

Bodhisattva

What does Bodhisattva Never Disparaging's profound respect for people signify? The purpose of the appearance in this world of Shakyamuni Buddha, the lord of teachings, lies in his behavior as a human being.

The Three Kinds of Treasure[1]

The twentieth chapter of the *Lotus Sutra* tells the story of Bodhisattva 'Never Disparaging', a man with profound respect for all humanity. He bows to everyone he meets on his travels – even those who try to harm him. When he is attacked with stones he simply retreats to a safe distance before once more bowing to his persecutors:

I deeply respect your life because you, like me, have Buddhahood.[2]

The ignorant and arrogant, even the violent, are all acknowledged by him. He considers them worthy of respect, because they all possess Buddhahood. Believing in everyone's potential and working for their happiness no matter what: this is the life-state of bodhisattva.

I first learned of Bodhisattva Never Disparaging only a few weeks into my Buddhist practice. Hermione's ex-girlfriend, also a friend of mine, arrived at my office one afternoon, angry and upset. We argued about something, I can't remember what, but on reflection it must have been coloured by her feelings towards my new closeness with Hermione. She clearly felt betrayed and let down. I rose up in retaliation (uncontrolled, self-righteous anger) and before long we were shouting at each other. I demanded that she leave my office, which she refused to do, and as I tried push her out she sent me flying across the office floor in full view of my colleagues. Another one of my less than classy moments, and one that also left me thoroughly shaken.

Later, I sought out the leader of our local Buddhist group for guidance. A compassionate mentor, Rose explained how we practise to respect everyone, even if they are disrespectful towards us. That's when she told me about Never Disparaging, explaining that this bodhisattva spirit is how we create peace in the world.

'But we must always put ourselves at a safe distance', she added. 'Self-respect is paramount.'

I clearly needed to develop the wisdom to give certain people and situations a wider berth. I needed to respect my own life first.

Helping others is a natural human desire. A parent loves their child, a doctor or nurse cares for their patient, a teacher believes in their student. But the high life-state of bodhisattva requires more than an inbuilt yearning or good intentions. First, it is a conscious decision, moment by moment. Then wisdom, compassion and courage – the innate qualities of the Buddha – are needed every step of the way. Above all, bodhisattva requires conviction – an unwavering commitment to the belief in every single person's potential. Even then bodhisattva may reveal its negative aspect. Selflessly giving to others, if not carried out from a position of self-respect, can easily manifest as martyrdom or self-sacrifice. There is a thin line that separates pure-hearted altruism from 'giving too much'.

In the wake of Oz's passing, Jetman flew to Kovalam with a proposal. He wanted me to live with him in London. As we sat under the stars, the warm evening breeze carrying scents of exotic flowers to our table, he told me that as far as he was concerned we had arrived at our fairy-tale ending. Finding each other, he said, after all our respective challenges, was our mutual reward. Our destiny, he felt, was the gift of his deceased parents, whose spirits had conspired to bring me – the perfect partner – to him. As the lights of the fishermen's boats twinkled out at sea, and the cicadas crackled reassuring in the trees, he pledged his undying love. I felt so peaceful and safe. Did I dare to believe this was the happy ending I'd sought for so long? This man was so honorable, so gallant, such a gentleman, such a sweetheart…

I truly felt that my Prince had come.

We met a few days later in Bombay and stayed at the Taj Palace hotel, overlooking The Gateway of India, preparing for our flight home. I watched the sun rise out of the ocean as I began my morning practice, and the lilies on the table opened into full bloom as my heart expanded. That evening as we waited for our car to the airport, we lay in bed, comfortable now in each other's company, excited for the journey ahead. We had established early on in our friendship our shared passion for flying, discovering that we both kept every boarding pass in a special box. Tonight's boarding passes, we said, would be the most special of all.

And then suddenly, a hiccup, as significant as it was small. A text pinged on his phone, interrupting our peaceful conversation. It was from someone with whom he'd had a fleeting affair. But the text said that she had just left his apartment, watered the plants and left the keys on the sideboard. *What the…?!* They'd lived together. Up until today. *He'd never told me that!* My heart started to race. My stomach turned over. I rushed to the bathroom and tried to compose myself, but the trigger was pulled and the shot had been fired.

Jetman offered an explanation. That he'd let her stay in his spare room while she sorted things out. That he'd never loved her. That they were only friends. If he'd told me she was staying in his home it would have put our relationship at risk. There was nothing between them. He swore *on his daughter's life*. It was just me and him. No one else. There never would be anyone else. For ever and ever… Then he started to cry. He couldn't lose me now. Not for anything. 'We can't throw away what we have for such an insignificant mistake', he pleaded.

And because I wanted to believe him I took comfort in his words, and eventually relaxed into his arms. But deep in my heart I knew that a line had been crossed. Moreover, there was still a weakness within me that could disturb my peace of mind in an instant. The concierge called up with the news that our car was ready. It was time to fly. In truth, we were already off the ground.

Jetman lived up to his name once again that night when he took me into the cockpit of the plane that flew us home. I sipped tea with the captain as she welcomed me into the jump seat whilst steering the five hundred passengers behind us back to my homeland. It was surreal. Later, as I closed my eyes, I let the gentle swaying of the aircraft and the distant hum of its engines rock me into comforting dreams, a white horse carrying me across the ocean with my new love holding the reins.

As the weeks unfolded I realized how much help Jetman needed. He gave a lot, but he asked a lot too. Within a fortnight he'd travelled back to India on business and asked me to start making his bare apartment into a place we could call home. Sometimes I stumbled across the possessions of his ex-girlfriend, and my heart would race when the mail arrived with her name on yet another utility bill. As the weeks went by it became apparent they'd lived there as a couple. 'She was just here doing my administration', he would say, when I confronted him. 'Please relax. This is your home now.'

When Jetman was in London he would shower me with affection and gifts, always demanding my undivided attention. Yet his trips were spontaneous. 'Three days' often turned into three weeks, as his responsibilities in India took longer than anticipated. 'Things will change', he would say. 'It's just going to take a little time.'

Sometimes I travelled with him, but our trips to India together became a fresh breeding ground for my insecurity. He always stayed in his family home, where his estranged wife and daughter lived, whereas I was accommodated in a hotel across town. He never spent a full night with me, returning in the early hours to his house and wishing me goodnight from his single bed by phone. I felt selfish and weak for how deeply this bothered me, for failing to appreciate the difference in our cultures or to take into consideration the feelings of his daughter, whom he was desperate not to upset. He invited me for dinner so that I could meet her, but I was forbidden to refer to our relationship, taking my place at the family table in an undefined capacity. Had I, like the Little Mermaid, sacrificed my tongue for the sake of this relationship?

'Give it time', he said. 'I want you to be a mother to her. One day she will love you as much as I do.' Oh the irony! Once I had considered Jetman some sort of reward for not having settled for 'Life's' compromise. Yet here I was, hardly one step further. How I wished I had come further than this…

If there were one word to sum up what I felt in these moments, it would be 'shame'. That weakness within me which fueled my self-doubt, created guilt and then turned me in on myself. I was guilty of jealousy. Shame on me. I was guilty of impatience over his pressing schedule of commitments and responsibilities. Shame on me. I was ungrateful for his generosity and unflagging devotion. Shame on me.

And so, as my guilt and shame increased, so did my determination to find a solution, to make this work. I decided I must accept Jetman's shortcomings and focus instead on transforming my own. *I have to give more. I have to open my heart. I need more compassion. I need to grow...* Already I was teetering on that line between bodhisattva and co-dependent.

In our early days of friendship I had made it clear I still wanted to have children. Jetman had assured me it was fine, something that he was happy to contemplate, but after six months of being together he recanted and said his personal circumstances would not allow it. If having children was non-negotiable I would have to rethink our relationship. Should I finally accept that becoming a mother was not for me? *Who was I to parent a child?* Shame once again. I retreated to my house to think things through. But he drove over and refused to leave until I went back home with him. Needless to say I yielded.

By way of compensation, Jetman insisted that we got a puppy. He found a litter of standard black poodles and we drove out to Norfolk to see them. I already had a name in mind and when I went into the enclosure where the six-week-old puppies were playing, one of them ran straight up to me and sat down very politely. She looked up at me with sparkly almond-shaped eyes.

'Oh! So *you're* Lottie, are you?' I said knowingly.

I picked her up and held her close. As we chatted with the breeders, Lottie fell fast asleep on my lap. All at once I was a puppy mummy. And there was no love like it.

Having Lottie around made up for the times that Jetman was away. It also restricted me from travelling with him. My hands were full with feeding, training, walking, playing. Lottie would always sit with me while I chanted, usually snuggling up on my lap and falling asleep. My prayers at this time were for our collective happiness. I chanted for Jetman to resolve his family issues. I chanted for his daughter to feel absolutely secure and happy. I chanted for a home where we could all live happily together. During one of these chants, Jetman came flying out his office excitedly waving a piece of paper.

164

'I've found us a house to live in!' he declared. His eyes sparkled as he danced around.

'What do you mean? We already have a house to live in!'

'But you must see this house. It's amazing!'

I looked at the description, which he had pulled off the Internet.

'Call and get us an appointment!' he said. 'This has to be the home where we spend the rest of our lives together...'

'So it will be *our* house then?' I asked. 'You want us to buy this together?'

'Yes, of course! It's for you, me and Lottie. This is our home. I want to die there with you.'

When Jetman decided he wanted something, he invariably got it. I missed my house in West London, and this one was not dissimilar, albeit in a smarter part of town. Surely this was the catalyst for life to settle down.

'All right.' I said, joining his eagerness. 'Let's go for it!'

A painful negotiating process ensued, which I salvaged at every step. It began with Jetman's offer being refused. So I delivered a handwritten letter to the owners, stating the case for why we would be the perfect buyers. The owner was oddly amused as I stood in his drive in the pouring rain, handing him my missive, Lottie in my arms and a black cab waiting at the gate. He accepted our offer and I took the purchase through to exchange of contracts within 28 days. For all of this time Jetman was in India, shouting his orders across a phone line that repeatedly dropped during the conversation. Stress and adrenaline left me feeling weary. He seemed to thrive on it.

Gina was getting sicker by the day. She had embarked on a relentless course of chemotherapy since her diagnosis a few months before. I sometimes took her to the clinic and sat with her while she received treatment. She would ask about Jetman and our life together. Although she'd never met him, she was always full of questions and encouragement. Gina's cancer was intense, never letting up for a moment, but she always put a brave face on it. She was determined to recover, even as her health deteriorated rapidly over those summer months.

Who was I to complain about the pressures of my life? They were insignificant in comparison. Maybe relationships were always going to be hard work, because of my history, because of my experiences. *Things will get easier in time*, I thought. *Things will settle down.*

At the end of the summer I insisted that Jetman and I took a break together. He had been working so much that we'd seen little of each other. We drove to the South of France, to Provence, stopping off at various hotels en route. Yet he took along a legal document that he read constantly for the first three days. We had only just arrived at our hotel on the beach when he declared we needed to go back to London immediately for urgent business. I was really looking forward to a rest, but suddenly, it seemed, we were off again. I was furious.

'You're a cunt', I said.

I was really upset.

Memories of the misery-go-round came flashing back. Serenity was at threat. My peace of mind was disturbed, and in the process I had become Bodhisattva *Most* Disparaging.

I apologised straight away, horrified at my outburst. Jetman apologised too, and we vowed to put it behind us. We drove back to London with what felt like a new understanding. He took the wheel for the entire journey, which we did in one hit, stopping only for petrol. Cap d'Antibes to Central London in ten hours. He shone with adrenaline. It was the way he liked to live.

'Let's all go to Kovalam in December', he said. 'Let's take a crowd. Invite Sara and Tony and your godchildren. Ask Mary and Laiya to come too. I'll pay for everyone. Let's have a ball!'

And so, life with Jetman went on.

For all that the fairy-tale romance was beginning to curdle, my faith and practice remained strong, which provided a positive framework for viewing challenges. Changing karma is the bodhisattva's mission. Problems are there to be transformed into opportunities; otherwise we'd never be able to help others do the same. With this attitude, the tendency to resent life's challenges diminishes. Every day I chanted to resolve my weaknesses, to continue growing, and to change any poison I encountered into medicine.

I regularly practised with the Buddhists in our local area. Being part of a community of practitioners, or *sangha* as it is traditionally known, is considered an essential training ground for changing karma. My *sangha* had originated in Japan in the 1940s as an expression of peaceful rebellion against the prevailing military dictatorship. In the ten years after the Second World War almost a million practitioners had arisen from the deadly shadow of Hiroshima and Nagasaki, creating a counter-force to the atrocities of war. By the time I joined, there were over twelve million practitioners in 190 countries worldwide.

Being part of a community of 'fellow bodhisattvas' provided both a learning environment and a place to resolve the inevitable irritations and frustrations that come with diversity. In the early days of my practice I saw how my impatience could be projected towards people who spoke too much at meetings, or in accents that were difficult to understand. And I soon grew to realize that this was the point. My frustration towards other people's differences and seeing my own shortcomings in full glare were the fuel for change. Right here in this room, I had everything I needed to become a better person. Intolerance towards someone else is just another opportunity to develop compassion and deepen belief in their potential.

After that first year with Jetman I was asked to take on a leadership responsibility in the local *sangha*. I was deeply moved. How much I had grown in the ten years since I had first met Margie and stared at her, wide-eyed in my fearfulness and confusion. Despite all my current frustrations I had come a long way, and accepting this new role felt like a staging post. Going through personal evolution can be uncomfortable but it's what life's about. If we don't face difficulties, how can we expect to grow?

It was early December and I was preparing a study lecture. As I made my way to the lecture hall Gina's partner called and said I should come to the hospital soon. *There won't be much time.* That night I dedicated my lecture to Gina. It was based on a teaching called the 'Sutra of True Requital',[3] which narrates the story of the Dragon King's Daughter and explains the importance of believing in the enlightenment of all women. It also expresses appreciation for parents and for their gift of life. In particular it celebrates the mother. The nurturing quality of our Buddha nature is likened to a mother's compassion.

I had felt Gina's compassion throughout all the years of our friendship, and I reflected on her support, her belief in me, as I drove through the London streets to the lecture hall. I remembered her calm surety, her gentle wit and her vibrant zest for life. She was loyal, affectionate and protective. No one had been a greater support during my early years of recovery than Gina, who had stood by faithfully, always believing in me, even when I hadn't believed in myself. Gina had helped me become the person I was today and I pledged to carry her spirit in my heart as I formally took on my new responsibility that evening.

The next morning I woke early after a restless night and drove before dawn to the hospital. The streets were quiet. Even the West End was still sleeping. I hadn't seen Gina for a few weeks. Though hardly conscious she tried to sit up when I got to her bed. She knew it was me. Less than an hour later she passed away peacefully. She had waited.

For some time I stayed with her, chanting and holding her hand. As I sat there, I reflected on our youth, the innocence with which we'd met, and that 'knowingness' between us from that very first night when we were so familiar and comfortable with each other, to this moment now as I promised to meet again in our next life. I know that we will.

It was early December and the air was chill as I left the hospital. I felt empty, a soulmate missing on this earth. Nothing fills the gap of losing a loved one. You just lose them, and you go on without them. Oh, the innocence of youth! Those exciting early days with your life ahead of you, when you have absolutely no idea where it is all heading, not even thinking about how you will eventually part, how you will say your goodbyes. And then here you are, still feeling as young as you were back then, and you really are saying *goodbye.*

Grief hit me hard but I kept it close tight as climbed off the plane at Trivandrum, disappointed to be arriving alone once again at the hotel in which Jetman and I had forged our love only a year before. As Gina's funeral took place in London, I sat alone on the balcony terrace looking out to sea. The sky was the deepest blue, all the flowers were in bloom, and colourful butterflies danced in the air. I chanted for three hours, praying for Gina's eternal life with all my heart. Here I was, back in my spiritual home. The year that had begun with Oz's departure was now ending with Gina's. And for all my strength and hope for the future, in that moment I felt desperately sad and alone.

Jetman was busy preparing for his horseracing event and after a week I flew to Bombay to meet everyone: Sara, Tony and the godchildren, Aunt Sue and Uncle George, and Laiya, who had travelled alone to be with us. Having them there with me was a blessing, after all the times before when I had sat in the family box, alone. This time Jetman's daughter brought her mother, who sat close by, watching with contempt and throwing disapproving looks. My 'family' however, rallied round, especially Laiya who seemed to empathise the most. She followed me to the bathroom when I needed to take a breath.

'I want to leave', I told her.

'I don't blame you', she said.

When I told Jetman that I wanted to go back he begged me to stay so I did, but we ended the night on an argument back in my hotel room. He couldn't understand why the situation was uncomfortable, not just for me but for everyone. It felt as though the gap was widening between us and whatever I said only seemed to make things worse.

The next day we all flew to Trivandrum. Everyone stayed for a week and an atmosphere of togetherness blossomed. I swam with my godchildren in the swimming pool at night. By day I went for walks and sat with Laiya on her balcony, chatting gently about the loss of her sister two years before. Sue and George joined us for a great Christmas Day lunch at a restaurant on the beach. Yet I felt distant from Jetman – as though I was being pushed away. Sometimes I became jealous of his attention to Sara and Laiya, who, it seemed, could do no wrong. They were 'gracious women', he said; Sara the 'elegant and exceptional mother', Laiya 'sweet and demure'. *Shame on my insecurity*, I thought, as I told myself to be more generous and to celebrate abundance with this complex partner and precious family and friends.

Back in London I decided to put all my energy behind a project to set up Jetman's retail premises. He presented the idea as an answer to my future security and asked me to head the operation. 'This belongs to you', he said. I thought that helping him realize one of his dreams whilst creating something together would improve things between us. So I brought together my experience and contacts from the brand design world and embarked on a mission to make it successful. *If I can make this good*, I thought, *I will secure Jetman's respect and love. I can mend things. I can fix it.*

I was back in the classroom of 1977.

The lease on the premises had already been signed so I was up against the clock to get the shop open. Days turned into nights. I rarely took a break. And I was in it on my own. Jetman spent more time in India than he did in the UK, and whenever he came over he brought an old friend with him. We had very little time together. And I was exhausted. I had directed every aspect of the project: architects, designers, building contractors, brand, staff, training, marketing, everything. As the launch day drew close, Jetman was in India and I wasn't even sure if he would be there on the day. He did come back in the end. But his affection towards me ran hot and cold.

Laiya would call me regularly and I confided in her a lot. She was very supportive and always had an opinion on the difficulties I faced, making it very clear that Jetman was being unreasonable.

'I couldn't do it', she said, reassuringly. 'Put your foot down!'

At the end of the summer we both joined Mary for a girls' weekend at her family home in Spain. It was an oasis. Exhausted from overworking and parched from the lack of emotional support at home, I drank deep from the waters of sisterly conversation with close female friends, and shared with them my deepest fears and insecurities. *For all of life's challenges,* I thought, as Laiya and I practised handstands on the grass one hot sunny afternoon, *I am so fortunate with the friends I have made along the way.*

The next two months were a whirlwind, Jetman now insisting that I run the business day to day. And there was another issue to face as the house sale neared completion. It was time to move.

I'd been thinking for a while that Jetman and I should part ways. There was a widening gap between us that I couldn't explain. Something just didn't add up. It was as if there was part of the picture I couldn't even see. I put it down to my lack of wisdom and chanted for a resolution, to see the right way forward. Jetman, however, reassured me that we would resolve all our differences and that I should get everything in place for the move. I wanted to remain loyal to our commitment. There had to come a point where I could see a relationship through. Yet emotionally and physically I was flagging. To execute an entire house move felt like another Herculean task. I did it, of course. Spinning plates had become my specialty.

October 23rd was the two-year anniversary of our first date. On the same day a large removal van deposited all our possessions to our new address. Yet, on what should have been one of the happiest days of our lives, misery slunk in. Jetman glared moodily as he walked around the house, scowling at every suggestion I made. Then he said we couldn't stay there because it wasn't 'an auspicious day'. *Bullshit*, I thought. One week later, he finally broke off the relationship. He needed to 'focus on his daughter', he said. *Bullshit*, I thought again.

For all his promises, for all the insistence that I must never leave him, with all my personal things sitting in our new home and with my professional life entrenched in a business that we jointly owned, Jetman had cut the engines without so much as an apology.

A thousand of the heaviest bucketfulls of deepest darkest *shame on me...*

I had to fly to New York the very next day, from where I would carry on to Nashville, Tennessee. Bright Lady had recommended I go to a place called Onsite Workshops and the trip had been planned for some time. As the aeroplane lifted into the sky I struggled to come to terms with the previous night's revelation. *We were no longer a couple. We were no longer living together. Everything had changed.*

I had always loved long flights. I love the way that time becomes surreal, almost nebulous, as time zones and flight times fight their way through a logical argument that leaves the passenger confused, in a world apparently so small that it can be measured in a few units of hours. Today I took solace in the space that the flight created, a welcome limbo-land as time effectively stood still, where nobody could touch me, reach me or hear me. Yet, as my thoughts were set free, a cacophony of voices surged in my head, crashing like waves in an angry sea.

This can't be happening. How can I be here? How was I so wrong? After everything I've done. I've failed. Big time. I'm so ashamed. How could he do this? This wasn't the plan. What am I going to do? And one thought that stood out above all the others: Y*ou need a strategy. You have to turn this around.* That was the voice of my survivor. Working out the next step. *Where do we go from here?*

But in that moment, somewhere between England and America, hanging in a pocket of time and space mid-Atlantic, I honestly did not have a clue. I think the tears came at this point, prompted by a benign rom-com on the small screen in front of me, reflecting my inadequacies, pulling on my heartstrings. I was completely defeated.

In New York it was Halloween night and the Upper West Side was decorated in style. Ghosts, witches, cobwebs and pumpkins adorned the streets while children ran excitedly between the houses, dressed in costumes as absurd as my life. I was still in a daze when I landed at Nashville the following day, a sense of disorientation exaggerated by the sight of rocking chairs in the airport, and the sound of clichéd country music songs playing in the Arrivals hall: *D-I-V-O-R-C-E...*[4] As I waited for the bus that would take us to the Onsite facility at Cumberland Furnace I shrank from my fellow travellers, recoiling from their attempts to pull me into conversation. I hated everyone. *What was I doing here? Leave me alone. Don't come near me.* Another two hours and we arrived at our destination in the middle of nowhere, surrounded by forests and hills. It was like a movie playing somewhere in the distance, a pale shelter for my fragile, disconnected heart.

For the first twenty-four hours I dived into washrooms, sobbed for a while, tried compose myself, then crumbled the minute I came out. But gradually, once the work had begun, I started to get a sense of what it was all about, and found myself giving into it quite quickly. 'Trust the process', we were told. *What the hell? What did I have to lose?* Absolutely nothing.

My work in the small group was to understand the thoughts or the voices in my head, the chorus of confusion that had deafened me during my flight and, I now realized, sabotaged every close relationship since childhood. It was time to intervene. With the help of my therapist and the people in my group, I was able to put a name to each thought pattern. Having done so I discovered that, underneath all the stronger voices, the ones that drove me, the ones that judged and blamed, there was a central voice, a little voice, the 'me' of eight years old.

I'm bad. I'm dirty. I don't deserve love.

This little voice defined the broken-heartedness that I took with me into relationships. It was the voice that lovers and partners were drawn to, attracting people maybe with a similar voice of their own – or conversely those who could take advantage of my vulnerability.

Then I was encouraged to draw images that expressed a reversal of these self-defeating voices, affirmations that would counteract my shame. So I sketched clear blue water: *I am clean.* I drew abundance: *All my needs are met.* The voice of criticism became the voice of reason, a clear ambition for a mutual, healthy and respectful attraction between me and another person: *Be safe, take it slowly.* And my strategy? *Self love.* I pictured a big beautiful heart with a smiling face…

And I remembered a Buddhist teaching: *Employ the strategy of the Lotus Sutra before any other.*[5] The strategy of the *Lotus Sutra*: self-respect and self-esteem – then extend this outward in respect and esteem for others. Self love.

As the week went on, I slowly put myself back together again with the help of my group. I was able to focus on the essential part of me, deeper than my karma, greater than all the wounds and trauma and all the negative things that had affected me in life. I connected with my spirit, my true self, my Buddha nature. I laughed. I encouraged. I loved.

Walking in deep meditation one morning, out on a hill overlooking a Tennessee valley, I sensed that the voices in my mind had changed. *I am clean*, they said. *All my needs are met. I can love myself.* In that moment, as the sun rose above the trees, its light transforming the dew on the grass into a million diamonds, I promised myself again that I would always love myself, as I am, no matter what.

I fell sick soon afterwards and lost my voice completely, as though my inner demons were activated, trying to sabotage my progress. It didn't matter. I trusted the process even more and focused on listening rather than talking, sharing my group members' work with a newfound compassion. As I did, I grew in confidence at the prospect of returning to my new life back at home. Not only could I do this, it was going to be for the best. This was a new start.

In spite of my physical sickness, which was strengthening at an alarming rate, I felt spiritually and mentally strong. And as I bid my group goodbye, I made a determination:

This experience will not be the breaking of me. Rather, it will be the making of me.

Back in London I called out a doctor in the night, panicking as I vomited from coughing so much, my temperature raging.

'You have whooping cough', the doctor said. 'Didn't you have it as a child?'

A childhood disease! I had caught a childhood disease as I'd found my childhood voice. *I must be on the right path!*

It was late autumn. As I walked Lottie in the early morning darkness, strong winds blew leaves from the trees in thousands. Broken-heartedness ran through me as I grieved heavily for love that was lost. There it was again, the desolate feeling that had accompanied me through life. It felt like a hallmark, ingrained in my heart. *Was I destined to be alone?*

Pain took my breath as I looked up to the stormy sky and watched the trees swaying, their falling leaves illuminated by the street lamps. I felt completely 'out there' too, a solitary figure, separate from everyone, heading into the unknown, alone.

Freefalling, I thought. *I am freefalling. But where is my parachute?*

Faith is your parachute, my wisdom said.

Reassured, I smiled.

Kovalam was painful that year. 'Life' was back at home only briefly from working in Germany where he now ran huge IT programmes for a large insurance company. He told me, as we sat outside and talked one evening, our faces lit only by the moon and the stars, that every month when his salary arrived he thanked the Universe for me, because I had encouraged him and helped him believe what was possible. As I recounted what had happened since we had last spoken, my tears flowed. He was gently compassionate, upset for me, and angry with Jetman. Then he told me that his life was now everything that he wanted it to be, but that there was one thing missing. Me. I was clear this time.

'You would need a divorce certificate and a UK visa before we could even start to have that conversation', I said.

'It will take me five years to get both', he said.

For a short time I relaxed, trusting 'Life' as I lay my head on his legs and looked up at the stars. I exhaled, glad to be in the company of a man I could trust. Our connection went far beyond romance. Ours was a friendship that was based on respect and the truth.

'You are strong and you are beautiful', he said, as he gently stroked my hair. 'Life goes up and down. In fact, the downs create the ups. Don't worry. Everything's going to be OK.'

I pressed forward, pushing myself through the early mornings and the intense yoga practice, determined to leave my grief behind. *I can do this,* I told myself. *I am strong. Just move forward. It's for the best. Life goes on.* Two days before leaving I pushed myself too far. On a day when I should probably have rested in bed, I dislocated my knee during practice – only for a moment before it clicked back into place, but it was enough. There was no doubt that teenage trauma was surfacing again. I was thrown completely off balance. Rosanna, one of Lino's teaching assistants, observed, 'You don't go through that kind of emotional upset without it having an impact somewhere in your body.' She was absolutely right. It showed me what was still unresolved, and I returned to London with an uneasy feeling that my darkest demons were yet to be faced.

The year hadn't started well. I limped off the plane, not sure which part of me was the most sore. It was a cold winter with snow on the ground, and I carried on at the business, staring at the computer screen, resenting it more and more each day. This wasn't my dream; it was Jetman's. And here was I, making it happen for him, not even his partner now, and relying on it for income. *This karma of mine!*

And then, finally, a moment of revelation when Jetman called me one day to access his bank account. After he'd hung up the phone I glanced back at his statement. Three transactions leapt off the screen. That very week Jetman had been at my friend Laiya's three favourite restaurants…

Maybe she's doing some work for him, I thought.

'Have you seen Laiya recently?' I asked when he came in later.

'No', he said. 'Not at all.'

'Really? So you haven't even heard from her?'

'No, why should I have?'

'No reason', I said. 'I haven't seen her either. I'll give her a call.'

I didn't believe him, of course. Jetman never seemed to tell me the truth, and I had a suspicious feeling now that wouldn't go away.

'Ask your friend', said Bright Lady a few days later when I brought it up.

So I called Laiya and we arranged to meet. We walked Lottie around Hyde Park in the sunshine, sharing close conversation as we always had. We were nearing the end of our walk by the time I brought up the subject. It was awkward, not an easy thing to ask a friend.

'I need to ask you something', I said.

'What is it?'

'I have a feeling that you and Jetman have been seeing each other.'

'Whatever made you think that?' she said so sweetly that I felt awful for having even asked the question.

'I saw his bank statement', I said. 'He'd been to your favourite restaurants. Three of them in a week.'

She stared at me blankly.

'Am I being paranoid?' I asked.

'Yes, absolutely', she replied.

A few days later, my phone provider sent Jetman's phone bills and mine for the last twelve months so that I could finalise the company accounts. *Don't snoop,* I told myself. *You asked Laiya directly. Believe that she told you the truth.* So I scooped the files into a directory. They could wait there for now.

A few weeks after that I was at my desk. There was a press event going on and the place was full of journalists and guests. I was supposed to be out there mingling, but I was weary of it all and had retreated to the office where Lottie was curled up asleep beside my chair. A nagging thought pressed on me as I flicked between the programmes on my screen. *What was I looking for?*

My eyes moved to the directory of phone bills that I still hadn't opened.

Just open a couple, I thought. *Prove your paranoia, then lay it to rest.* Randomly I opened one and scanned the list of Jetman's calls and texts. At the same time I opened Laiya's number on my phone and searched for a match.

At first I thought I must have been looking at a recent bill, judging by the frequency with which Laiya's number featured on Jetman's account. Six texts, three texts, and a ten-minute call, all in one day. Then I realized that I wasn't looking at a recent bill. I was looking at one from a year ago, only months after our holiday in India.

My eyes pored over the page, my heart pounding faster.

I opened another bill, again from last year, while Jetman and I were still living together and I was working those twelve-hour days setting up the business.

Ten texts, seven texts, three calls.

My mouth went dry and my heart beat even faster.

I reached for my phone, frantically scrolling through texts from Jetman, reminding myself of their content whilst identifying them on his bill too. Quite clearly I wasn't the last person he had messaged before his flight took off on those many trips away. I could also see the time he spent talking to Laiya while I was walking Lottie or after I had left to go to work, and how he would often message her before coming to bed with me. They had spent hours on the phone while I was away sometimes, even after Uncle George passed away. Finally. It was all too clear. Jetman really *was* a cunt!

Yet it was Laiya's betrayal that bit the deepest. For Jetman to lie was almost expected, but from her it was unbearable. All the time my trusted friend had been manipulating and controlling events. She had duplicitously gleaned privileged information during our many confidential conversations and used it for her own ends. By the time Laiya and I were doing handstands in the garden in Spain, there had been masses of texts and calls between them. And, as soon as Jetman had finally broken things off with me, I could see how their contact exploded into

179

a day-in, day-out frenzy of constant communication that was still going strong. I flicked between my computer screen and my phone in disbelief.

How could you? I messaged Laiya.

Silence.

Of course she knew what I meant.

My heart raced and my stomach was on fire, gripped with a sickening fury that could have launched me from the chair. This was the same white-hot rage that I had hit at the Priory on Trauma Week. The anger of betrayal.

Adrenaline coursed through my veins.

Never mind fight or flight, I wanted to kill or die.

Kill or die.

Anger and shame.

My thoughts were murderous. I pictured holding Laiya's head at the bottom of the Serpentine Lake at the very spot where she had led me to believe that I was paranoid when I'd asked her for the truth. It tormented me. *How could she do this? How could she do this? How could she?!*

And then, when the anger eventually subsided, shame erupted. An avalanche, a tsunami, a dark surging tidal wave of deep dark shame that swept me away.

Shame. On. Me.

And with that a desperate feeling of wanting to give up, completely, once and for all.

Throw yourself into the waves, Little Mermaid. You deserve nothing more.

I wanted to die.

Slander. The root cause of unhappiness. Self-doubt. Self-hatred. Anger. Resentment. Ignorance. It all lay before me. I was seething with betrayal, blinded with self-loathing. Yet, if I aspired to the bodhisattva way, I must turn this around. No matter what anyone else had done, only I was responsible for changing the way I felt. I knew where I wanted to get to – a place of warmth and compassion and respect – but it resided in such a far-off place it felt utterly unobtainable. *How could I get to there from here?*

And then finally another thought. And with it some relief.

What if this relationship between Jetman and Laiya really was their sanctuary, the ultimate relationship of their lives? The tension in my body eased slightly. *What if theirs really was a match made in heaven?* For the first time in hours, anger subsided. *Hang on a minute. Is this some relief from my torment?* I didn't want this thought to be the answer, but there was no denying that it brought some respite, a momentary calm. *Perhaps something good could come out of this after all, something of value.* The pulsating feeling of vengeful hatred began to subside and I started to feel more like myself. I breathed a sigh of relief. I hadn't acted out. I hadn't lost the plot. I'd kept my shit together.

I told Bright Lady about it a few days later.

'You're absolutely right', she said. 'Wish for another what you would wish for yourself.'

So I went to town with it, imaging a love affair for them like no other. I pictured turquoise waters, sunlight refracting through glistening droplets in a heaven-sent paradise of golden sun and azure skies. I imagined hands held tight as the Orient Express meandered through mountains and valleys. I saw deserts and oceans and two lovers standing side by side, united in their love. It calmed me down. It stopped me from doing crazy things that would have put me in the wrong. It helped me raise myself above the sordid betrayal of which they were guilty.

I wished for them what I wished for myself.

It's time to get out of here, I thought, and I turned to type out my letter of resignation.

Chapter Ten

Buddhahood

If you wish to free yourself from the sufferings of birth and death you have endured from time without beginning and to attain, without fail, unsurpassed enlightenment in this lifetime, you must perceive the mystic truth that is originally inherent in all living beings.

On Attaining Buddhahood in This Lifetime[1]

What is Buddhahood? What is enlightenment?

For all that has been written over hundreds of years, this is a life-state that is to be experienced rather than described.

For me, in the most simple terms, Buddhahood is a source of pure positive energy that resides within. I practice to connect with this energy as much as I can. When aligned with it, I am enlightened. When not aligned, I am deluded. One feels great – easy, focused, clear. The other feels awful – uneasy, unfocused, unclear. That's how I know if I'm connected, by how I feel, moment to moment.

Enlightenment is unconditional. It is the joy of simply being alive. It is a sense of freedom and indestructible happiness, very different from happiness that depends on the fulfillment of desires or the achievement of conditions. And the very best thing: enlightenment is a universal law that holds true for everyone, without exception. An enlightened person knows this. They realize their connectedness with all people, with all sentient beings, with all phenomena. In this respect, enlightenment is to know that we are all One.

It had been a long winter stretching endlessly into a cruel spring. Now, as summer cast its warmth, the revelation of betrayal still burned deep. In spite of wishing Jetman and Laiya well, wanting for them only what I wished for myself, no matter how much I prayed to respect their lives I was hurt. Deeply hurt.

A Buddhist friend caught my tears one weekend as I sobbed in her arms, choking on the force of emotion. It was the kind of snot-coming-out-your-nose, uncontrollable kind of crying, triggered by a deeper, older pain.

How could he do this? How could she? How could I have been so wrong?

Neither Jetman nor Laiya had apologized. Quite the opposite.

'You're deluded', Jetman said, raging at me soon after I'd fired my *How could you?* text at Laiya. 'Laiya and I are the best of friends! We have done nothing wrong!' My delusion would motivate me to *destroy his company from within*. I reassured him, I had no such goal. I just wanted to leave.

'You can't leave!' he said.

'This is harassment', I stated. With this he exploded.

'Are you threatening me?' he screamed. 'I will break you. I will see you thrown out of your own country. You are mentally ill. You need psychiatric help.'

'I respect your life', I said.

If I'm honest, I didn't really. But I had to start somewhere. I had attracted this situation into my life. So it was my responsibility to change it for the better. For now, I had one pressing concern: to respect and protect my own life by getting as far away as I could. I sought legal advice and began working my contractual notice period. I would be out of there by Christmas.

There was a summer reprieve while I took a holiday with Aunt Sue. She had come up with a plan to mark the painful anniversary of Uncle George's passing. 'I want to be snorkeling in a beautiful sea', she said. After some deliberation we settled on the Red Sea, deciding to ignore the diplomatic status of South Sinai, which had been declared 'Essential Travel Only' by the Foreign Office because of terrorist attacks earlier in the year. I found a good hotel in Dahab, a place that apparently boasted some of the best scuba diving in the world. We both needed an escape to a haven of aquamarine. 'Let's have an adventure', Sue said. I had the perfect Aunt.

As the EasyJet plane idled on the runway at Luton Airport in preparation for take-off, I looked over at the private terminal from which I had flown with Jetman. In the seat next to me a young mother had her hands full, her two-year-old boy bouncing and fidgeting on her lap. In that moment, and with only a few cramped inches separating me from the seat in front, I truly couldn't have felt more comfortable or content. I was so much happier to be here right now than over there, on a private plane with Jetman. Even what I thought had been good moments with him had been revealed to be a sham. Now I had my freedom, my own heart and mind. Life was real. I kicked back and closed my eyes, immersing myself in the music on my iPod, travelling light, face free of make up, relaxed, with no pretentions. I was in a good mood with everyone, and the world smiled back.

It had been almost nine years since my first trip to Egypt, and I'd forgotten its powerful beauty. The early evening heat enveloped me as I stepped off the plane and drank in the spectacular view. The driver raced through a pass in the red-peaked mountains to where, in the deserts beyond, the oasis of Dahab awaited. And the water. I couldn't wait to get in the water. From the moment that I let the air out of my diving jacket and descended into the sea, finding my balance floating weightlessly, I was at peace. It was beautiful down there, and I lost myself amidst the fish and sparkling coral. What had kept me away for so long?

Sue had set up a snorkeling trip with one of the guides from the hotel. Mina. 'The first pharaoh of Egypt', he told us as our jeep bounced across the desert tracks along the coastline. He was a tall, attractive schoolteacher from Cairo, there for the summer. Well educated, he spoke really good English and was full of wit. After we'd snorkeled for a while we sat down for coffee, looking out across the beautiful empty bay, the turquoise water backed by ancient mountains.

I smiled at his choice of music. 'Massive Attack', I said, on hearing the first note. 'My favourite band.' Then we all shared our broken hearts: Sue's from losing George, his from a recent break-up, and mine from my recent 'betrayal.'

'Meet me for tea this evening?' Mina asked.

'Sure, why not.'

Sue had a headache.

'You go', she said.

That evening a full moon hung over the bay, casting the world in a silvery light. It was a super moon, larger than any I had ever seen. I felt I could almost reach out and touch it. The temperature stayed well into the thirties as we sat by the water's edge, exchanging stories into the night. Literature, films, music and life… We swapped views and laughed freely. And as we looked into each other's eyes, we recognised a familiarity that seemed to go back lifetimes. We just knew.

When he leant over to kiss me all I felt was love – nothing more, nothing less. This was how love should feel. It was natural and mutual. It came with a sense of togetherness, purity and youthfulness that reminded me of my teenage love with Russell or my college days with Orlando. Best friends and lovers. The perfect fit. I liked the way he appreciated music. I liked his social conscience around education and other issues. I liked the way he adored nature and the dramatic landscape that enveloped us. As we sat by the water on my last night he sang *'Cause you're a sky full of stars*[2] and I laughed with such happiness I felt my heart would burst. For the first time in months something felt possible. So I asked him what he would want for us in an ideal world.

'For us to live here together', he said without hesitating.

'Could I bring my dog?'

'Of course you could!'

The tourist police jumped on us later that evening when we tried to go back to my hotel room. I had no idea laws existed that could dictate how consenting adults spent their private time. Me, the British woman, with such a strong sense of entitlement to my 'rights', argued with the hotel management until I was sure they would take no action. A ridiculous moment followed some hours later, long after Mina had left. The hotel reception woke me up, accusing me once again of having 'Mr. Mina' in my room.

'There is no Mr. Mina in my room!' I emphatically stated. 'There is no Mr. Mina!' Then the irony struck me. No misdemeanour! Really? Was I *really* sure of that?

The following day, as we said our goodbyes in the hotel lobby, I promised to come back.

'Please', Mina said.

And on the first morning back in London I booked a return flight for the following week.

To fall in love in the Middle East at such a delicate time politically and personally was extraordinary. Yet it was what my heart needed and, looking back, I have no regrets. I travelled constantly during those summer months, spending as much time in Egypt as possible. With every visit Mina and I grew closer. Sitting on a rock together, diving into the coral-laden water, playing with the bubbles from the scuba divers below, searching for Lionfish or doing underwater somersaults, over and over again.

One day in particular stands out. A perfect day.

We set off early and rode on camels for hours around the cliff face, just the two of us, not another person in sight. Eventually we reached a small Bedouin settlement where we swam in translucent waters right at the shore's edge. The fish were in abundance, as colourful as they were varied, the coral untouched, vibrating with a luminosity that was indescribably magical. As we glided through the water, holding hands, our eyes connected as they always did through our masks, in perfect union, perfectly in tune. I watched his eyes widen in excitement as he saw a squid shoot behind me, releasing its black ink in billowy clouds that hung in the water long after it had disappeared from view. He was animated, truly awestruck by what he had seen. Never before had I felt so alive and so present with another human being.

As we rode back home into the sunset, Mina reached out for my hand, taking it in his as he pressed something into my palm.

'Is this romantic enough for you?' he said. It was a ring he'd bought in Cairo. 'It's pharaonic.'

We rode home in peacefulness, me chanting softly with the deepest gratitude for what life had brought. A molten sun dipped behind the mountains and the pink sky melted into a silver sea. We both agreed it was the day of our lives.

And then I realized, in that moment, that everything I had wished for Jetman and Laiya, everything I had imagined for them, had actually come true for me. I had wished for them what I wished for myself, and now it had manifested in reality.

Who wouldn't want it to last?

We discussed our options. Moving to Dahab was unrealistic. Egypt had suffered two military revolutions in three years. The climate was tough, the atmosphere tense. We were living under the radar, thanks to open-minded landlords who would let us rent their apartments without having to be married. His family in Cairo would never accept our relationship, he said. London was our best option. So we hired a lawyer to apply for UK clearance. For the time being, at least, we had hope.

In the autumn I went back to Onsite in Tennessee for another round of group therapy. As much as love had offered a reprieve, it had left other issues unresolved. In fact, it felt even more important that I face my inner demons. With Mina's potential arrival in London, I could feel a deep insecurity building. I still had something crucial to reconcile.

One day I expressed my frustration at not being able to move forward in my life, unclear as to what I should do next, and still unresolved about what had gone so wrong with me and Jetman and Laiya.

'Do you have any money here with you?' the therapist asked.

'Yes, it's in my room.'

'Go and fetch it.'

When I came back the therapist asked someone to represent Jetman. In the background he asked that someone else represent my junior schoolteacher.

'Give him your money', he said, gesturing to 'Jetman'.

As I handed over my dollars, 'Jetman' started to throw them away, sneering at me as they fluttered through the air. To my absolute horror the scenario excited me. It actually turned me on… *WTF?* I was shocked and appalled. How could this possibly be? But it was true. There was a thrill in this. In a heartbeat I crumpled with shame. My therapist handed me a mirror.

'Can you look in the mirror?' he asked.

'No way', I said weakly.

'Why not?'

'Because I hate what I see.'

This simple exercise revealed the thought patterns, the neural pathways that had developed during my formative years. Shameful though it was to admit, I was subconsciously attracted to relationships that were based on an exploitation of trust.

'The important thing now', my therapist said, 'is to make sure that your current relationship doesn't become this.' He gestured to the space where the realization had been acted out. I reflected on the situation with Mina. It was already less than ideal. He would have to leave his family and his country if his visa came through, and I would be his only support. I had a flash of insight and my heart sank. *Mina's visa will be refused*, I thought. *He's not meant to come.*

On the last day the therapist encouraged me to do what he called a 'full body scream'. 'This exercise can be life-changing', he said. 'I'd be interested to know what happens after you've left here.'

As I let out almost forty years of repressed anger and fear, the image of my schoolteacher appeared in my mind's eye. I screamed with rage over his betrayal, the way he had exploited my innocence for his perverse amusement.

HOW COULD HE DO THIS TO ME?!!!

After it was over I felt nothing. Nothing had changed.

But then, a few days later, in the cab travelling home from the airport, I received a phone call from the East Midlands police. It was an officer from the Criminal Investigation Department. They were following up a number of allegations of indecent assault against my schoolteacher. Would I be willing to talk to them?

The Universe had heard me.

After a long interview the police officer in charge of the investigation established that, even under the laws in place in 1977, I was a victim of indecent assault. Finally, after all this time, I could face the truth. I had been molested for an entire year, whilst only eight years old. A few days later I gave my formal statement. It felt empowering having two police officers meticulously recording a detailed account of what had happened during that dreadful time. At last I was being taken seriously. Finally, after all those years of doubt and confusion, I was being heard.

Yet nothing prepared me for how far this trigger would throw me back, re-activating my traumatised eight-year-old psyche. As much as I tried to hold myself through it, I was locked, unable to stop the internal trembling or the sickly feelings of fear and shame. As I worked through my final weeks in the business, having to face Jetman most days, the environment seemed to hold up a mirror to those awful classroom memories. What was then was now. Just as I'd tried so hard to win the approval and protection of my abusive schoolteacher, so I had tried to please this man in my adult life. And more than this, both had caused me to question my reality and doubt my truth.

The nightmares were the worst part, my dreams playing out hellish scenes of terror, murder and abduction. I would wake, drenched in sweat, often as early as 1 a.m., then spend the rest of the night shaking with anxiety until falling asleep around 4 or 5. What had once been yoga time now became two hours of shivering in bed, holding a pillow tightly while I mentally rallied myself into finding the strength to get up and face another day. One night I woke in such rigid terror that it was impossible to sleep. I went to chant but could only mouth the mantra once before curling up on the rug. This struggle seemed endless. Unbelievable. As I lay there I thought once again about dying. It was a comforting thought. At last, an end to the pain.

So I played the idea forward in my mind – this time seriously thinking it through – what it would really be like to take my own life. But what of all the work I'd done so far, my faith, my practice and my journey of recovery? Everything I had gone through, the battles I had fought, the lessons I had learned? It would all mean so little if I were to leave behind nothing but a tragic legacy. The girl who tried so hard but just couldn't win. How would my story inspire anyone? What of the bodhisattva mission to transform suffering into happiness? It would fail on every level.

It's not an option, I thought. *I have to change this.*

I went back to bed and managed to fall asleep. In the morning I woke up with a fresh determination to beat it once and for all.

I sought guidance again from a senior Buddhist leader. *Was my karma so deep that it was impossible to change?* He explained that, when we are having doubts it is because we are failing to look at life from the bodhisattva's perspective – that changing karma is our mission. He said that these are 'crucial moments' when we need to deepen our faith and that we can do so through our relationship with the mentor. The Buddha must have 'the heart of a Lion King', he declared, quoting Nichiren. Interestingly, I found that the Chinese character for 'lion' is made up of two characters. The first character means 'teacher' and the second character means 'child', 'disciple' or 'student.' When the teacher and student join together it is like a lion's roar, the sound that marks the king of all beasts.

As the flawed and destructive relationship with my schoolteacher resurfaced so vividly, buttressed by this advice I turned afresh to the words of Daisaku Ikeda:

> *The key is courage. It is courage, and at the same time, the fundamental life force that wells forth in our lives when we summon up courage. More simply, it is the latent strength we possess within us. When we bravely struggle to protect the Law, the power of our courage dispels the mists of fundamental delusion that shrouds our hearts and allows the limitless power of the Law to flow from our lives. We reveal the life state of Buddhahood that is one with the Mystic Law.*[3]

Transformation starts with finding the courage to face our challenges. In confronting our greatest fears we open the door to our greatest potential. Courage is the springboard for even greater strengths to emerge. I had to be brave. I had to face these wounds of my childhood if they were ever to be healed.

I turned to further inspiration:

When your very life is at stake you struggle with every single ounce of your energy. But the battle against your own karma is even harder than that. Life and faith are just the same. To think that you can get through 'some way or another' is not real faith at all. When you try so hard that the sweat runs off you in streams and you squeeze out the wisdom you didn't even think you had, then you can make the impossible possible.[4]

This particular passage from Richard Causton's book had never failed to encourage me. If I were truly serious about transforming my life, changing my karma and contributing to world peace, I had to exert myself with every cell of my body, as if my life depended on it. Because, actually, it did.

Then suddenly Lottie fell ill. She started to vomit uncontrollably and she couldn't eat or drink. I took her to the vet who immediately put her on a drip. She had developed a severe imbalance, which he diagnosed as neurological. She couldn't walk or sit without falling over and one morning she had a seizure and collapsed in my arms. I thought I was losing her but she held on while I drove her to a specialist animal hospital out of town. For days the neurologists there tried to reach a diagnosis, but every test they ran was clear. We had one last option, an MRI scan to see if she had a brain tumour. There was nothing else it could be, the vet said.

Overnight Lottie's condition worsened. She developed a permanent head tilt. Something seemed to be pressing on the nerve in her brain that controlled her balance. *But what was it?* I held her close before she went under the anaesthetic, scared that this was the last goodbye. And then I waited. An hour later, the results came back clear. All clear. There was no tumour. *So what was wrong with her?*

'Take her to Professor Farmer', Margie said when I called her from the hospital. Margie had told me about this man before, an eighty-year-old medical doctor who had moved away from Western medicine many years before and now practised a type of acupuncture. Instead of needles, however, he used a low intensity laser, which penetrated deeper and regenerated new cells whilst clearing away the dead ones. He had mastered his technique to heal numerous health conditions without the need for medication. Although he worked mostly with human patients, his skill also extended to animals.

'He even cured an elephant last week!' Margie said.

It took me ages to find where Professor Farmer lived. He was in the middle of the country and my satnav took me through villages and between fields that I thought might turn into farm tracks if they became any more remote. Lottie was weak and frail and she fell over several times as we walked up the drive towards his house.

'Oh yes. We can sort that out!' Professor Farmer declared confidently as he looked at her.

'What is it?' I asked incredulously.

'It's a blocked nerve. We'll just clear it and she'll be fine. I bet the vets couldn't diagnose it, could they?'

'No, they couldn't', I said, reflecting on their huge bill for endless tests that had drawn nothing but blanks. Within minutes I watched the Professor locate a point in Lottie's spine that caused discomfort when he pressed it.

'Here it is!' he said, and took a photo of the inflammation beneath the surface using a thermal imaging device. He worked on Lottie with his laser for all of fifteen minutes.

'She'll be fine now. It will take a couple of days, and she'll be back to normal in a week.' Lottie relaxed and curled up asleep on the bed next to me.

I had a thought. Maybe, just maybe, this Professor could help me too. I took a deep breath.

'I have a problem', I said. 'And it's not that easy to explain.'

Leaving Professor Farmer's clinic, only one hour later, I felt profoundly different from when I had arrived. Calmer and clearer. My anxieties had eased away. As the familiar motorway lights stretched out before me towards West London, the Lucozade sign twinkled reassuringly as it marked my exit home. My heart lifted with hope. Was a physical intervention directly to my brain the essential piece of the jigsaw I needed to heal my trauma wounds of old?

It hadn't been easy, describing my condition to the Professor, but somehow I'd managed it.

'I was traumatised in childhood', I'd explained, 'particularly by a schoolteacher who indecently assaulted me for a year. Even now, when I get into relationships, I lose focus, panic and make painful choices. I lose my thinking...'

The Professor explained to me that there are particular receptors in the brain that deal with trauma and which, if they are overused, particularly in childhood, get clogged up with dead blood cells which then impair clear thinking. He showed me on his thermal imaging device. Significant areas of my brain were shaded with these cells. And then, just as with Lottie's blocked nerve in her neck, he used the cold laser to clear them.

'You'll think clearer now', he said. 'But there was a lot of congestion there. You may need a second treatment in a month's time.'

I smiled wryly as I considered the possibility that two of Professor Farmer's treatments in a month could take me further than eight years of addiction therapy. Of course it had taken eight years of addiction therapy to get me to the point where I could even articulate my issue to a complete stranger in two minutes without dissolving into a heap of shame. Even so, our meeting was still tinged with something of the miraculous. *Let's hope*, I thought. *Let's hope I've finally met a cure...* My head certainly did feel clearer.

That evening Lottie drank water by herself for the first time in weeks. The following day we went for a walk and she managed to stay on her feet as we delicately trod the familiar paths across Hyde Park. Within a week, just as Professor Farmer had predicted, she had made a full and complete recovery. It was astonishing.

At work, Jetman finally admitted that he and Laiya were together. I glanced at his laptop one day as I passed by his desk, his inbox full of emails from her.

'Just admit it', I said, speaking with a new-found confidence.

'It's true', he said, after a degree of squirming. 'We are together now.'

'And you called me deluded!' I walked out of the room.

What was the point in getting angry again? Nothing could change the past. They were together. They always had been. At least it was publicly acknowledged. The end of the year was approaching, and so was my departure from the business and his life. Soon I would be free.

My thoughts turned to the future with a new clarity and optimism. I'd had an idea. A seed had been sown in my mind, and every time I chanted, I watered the idea. Did it have shoots? It was a matter to discuss with Professor Farmer. Drawing on the guidance I'd read – *The key is courage* – I determined that I would talk to him about it on my next visit. It was incredible, this improvement I was feeling, my thinking so much clearer, my anxieties so much less intense. It was true, I had regained my focus, yes; but more than that I felt a new assertiveness. There was a calmness emanating from deeper within, and a desire to share this feeling with all the people I had met along the way. People who had suffered like I had. People who had experienced trauma and would keep recreating it, again and again. It made such practical sense that these brain receptors needed to be cleared. This physical treatment seemed like the missing piece of the jigsaw. Now I wanted to share this knowledge with others.

After Professor Farmer had cleared the last remnants of

the congested cells from my brain, I took a deep breath and broached the idea that had been forming in my mind. I wanted to learn how to do this. What did I have to do? Should I go to medical school? Would he teach me?

'I can see the way forward', I said. 'A new departure, an authentic path that feels right.'

'You have to know what you really want to do in life', said Professor Farmer. 'For me, I just knew that all I ever wanted to do was to heal. What do you want to do?'

'I want to relieve suffering', I said.

He nodded knowingly.

'Go to India and do lots of yoga, then come back in January and tell me for sure', he said.

I headed for India with a new-found determination. I knew what I needed to do. I was ready for it. With me I took two pieces of guidance. One was material for a lecture entitled 'The Difficulty of Sustaining Faith'.[5] The second was a book called *Healing and Recovery*,[6] written by the late David R Hawkins M.D., in which he shares years of research into the collective power of mind, body and spirit for healing. As I set out to find the answers more determinedly than ever, my heart and mind were open. I was willing to do whatever it took to change this karma of mine.

Returning to the same hotel as my first trip to Kovalam five full years before, I felt a sense of coming home. The familiar sounds and smells welcomed me back, the crows squawking above the seductive aroma of wood fires at dusk, and the sky casting its nurturing light across the balcony and into the very same bedroom. It was the perfect setting for my greatest piece of work, to connect with the fundamental truth: *I am the source of my own happiness.*

As the weeks passed, I realized how far my mindful and meditative practices, underpinned by my faith, were maturing. There was a naturalness to waking early and chanting morning prayers. Then, still before sunrise, I would make my way to the *yogashala* next door, joining with Lino and my yoga tribe in the Astanga mantra, our *Om* resonating freely through the darkness. Sometimes I would join my Buddhist *sangha* in Trivandrum for their weekly meetings, chanting together and sharing our mentor's guidance, my prayers extending throughout India and beyond – to friends and family in England and to all the people I was connected with around the world. I seemed to have developed a powerful combination now, the perfect platform for my inner work to flourish.

More than this, with heightened mental clarity I found it easy to focus on my studies. I voraciously devoured both books, reading them again and again until the pages grew dark under the barrage of pencil marks from my extensive notes. Free of encumbering waste, my brain cells leapt to attention. Study had never felt so liberating.

One day during practice Lino said to me,

'You are incredibly strong. Your body is strong.'

'But I have weak spots', I replied.

'Weak spots are in your mind', he said.

So true.

David Hawkins, like Daisaku Ikeda, places great emphasis on the importance of courage as the quality needed to move into the truth that we alone are the source of our power and that our happiness can only come from within. Hawkins discovered that once a person finds courage their life condition is propelled upwards into higher life-states associated with acceptance – love, joy, compassion, peace and eventually enlightenment. I was encouraged. This medical doctor seemed to confirm, on the basis of years of clinical research, what the Buddha had expounded in the *Lotus Sutra* over two thousand years ago: everyone is the source of their own power and everyone has the potential for absolute happiness. I knew already that chanting the title of this sutra, *Nam-myoho-renge-kyo*, would naturally reveal courage so I chanted once more to tap into the unlimited source that lay within me. As I did, not only did I reveal courage – wisdom illuminated where I needed to grow.

An enlightened person, I realized, doesn't view life in terms of right and wrong. Such a view is judgmental. It emanates more from the lower life-states of anger and ego than from wisdom or compassion. As I chanted with this in mind, I saw what a critical view I held of my life and the lives of others. How I had a tendency to view everything in black and white. How much I desperately needed to see Jetman and Laiya as 'wrong'. How desperate I was to be 'right'. I saw how sometimes the reverse sentiment took hold, as if they had somehow 'won' over me, while I was the 'low life' that 'deserved' their betrayal. Both views were judgmental; neither served me.

Once I had found the courage to see this truth I could move into the higher life-states of love and compassion. Everyone is at a different stage of being. Everyone has their own particular sufferings and challenges, their own unique karma. Through the gentle eye of compassion I understood more clearly that life just 'is'.

We are subject only to what we hold in our minds, Hawkins declares, with the unwavering certainty that we can even control the effects of pain, illness and injury if our thoughts are focused and strong.[7] I had always held other people responsible for my happiness. In this respect, I had always been deluded. I had given my power away, and my bitter feelings about other people's shortcomings had polluted my peace of mind.

As I looked deeper I saw that harbouring resentments towards others had served as a distraction from all the grievances I actually held towards myself. How many times had I subconsciously berated myself, abandoned myself, disrespected my life, held myself in low esteem, or let myself down? Never mind Laiya and Jetman, I had betrayed myself. Rather than waiting for them to apologise, I owed an apology to myself.

And from this revelation came an even deeper realization: *how could I forgive anyone if I didn't forgive myself first?*

I changed my prayer to focus on forgiveness: to forgive my critical nature, to forgive my judgmental attitude, to forgive myself for not being 'perfect', to forgive my lack of courage to face the truth, and to forgive myself for giving away so much self-respect as part of my misguided strategy for approval and validation. I chanted for forgiveness. And the more I forgave myself, the happier I became. It was the first step, preparing me for what came next – forgiveness for others.

It wasn't going to be easy, but I knew what I had to do.

It was a hot sultry evening. I had returned for a few nights to the hotel where I'd first stayed with Jetman and where we had all holidayed together two years before. In my mind's eye I sat Jetman and Laiya down beside me as I chanted, from my heart, to forgive.

As I chanted I connected with the desperate loneliness and need in Laiya to be loved. I saw how, in her naivety, she had felt justified in taking an opportunity that she thought would make her happy. Her life had been devoid of love, punctuated with trauma and abuse. This relationship, she must have thought, would provide her with happiness and security. In her yearning, our friendship had paled into insignificance. I forgave her betrayal. I let it go, and it set me free.

As I chanted some more, I turned to Jetman and reflected on the clouded love we had shared. I recognised the deep-rooted insecurity from which sprang his preposterous need to be in control of everything. I saw how much my harsh words had hurt him, his fragile ego too badly bruised to see beyond my frustration. In our vulnerability, right here in this very room, we had both bought into the fairy-tale ending three years before, neither of us prepared to acknowledge the consequences. As I forgave myself for my own delusion in love, so I forgave him, his shortcomings, his lies, his deceit, which, like a child's, had run untamed. I had learned so much. I appreciated everything that the relationship had brought. Now I could be thankful, put it to rest and move forward.

I thought of my parents, born into such difficult circumstances. They had not set out to cause me pain. On the contrary they had given me life. I was their flesh and blood. They had made sacrifices. They had supported me in every way they could. I had already forgiven them years earlier. Now I embraced them once more with a bigger heart and an even greater desire for their eternal happiness. Their karma, my karma, they were so close, so intertwined. To connect with my higher power was to change the course of our family karma – and with that to transform the sufferings of the delusion that we all shared.

And finally, my thoughts turned to my schoolteacher – the man lost in severe mental illness, guilty of such despicable behaviour, such gross abuse of helpless, innocent children. Yet, somewhere, deep in his life, beneath his illness, his karma, his delusion, I came to believe that there was a latent yet essential quality lying dormant. If the Buddha was correct, this sick man *must* have the potential to realize the severity of his behaviour. I prayed that he would confess and be placed by the authorities at a safe distance from other vulnerable children. I prayed that he would learn, face the consequences of his actions and change the course of his own karma.

But could I go one step farther? Could I forgive him for all he had done? Unless I forgave, I would be trapped by my resentment, still held in his power over me. I determined to become greater than his violation of me, refusing to let him define who I was. His illness would not be mine. And if I had the power to heal myself from this abuse, I also had the power to forgive. I also forgave everyone at that time for their failure to see, let alone address the problem: the headmaster, the other teachers, and the parents, including my own. Delusion had prevailed. They had not known. Ultimately, I had to forgive everyone if I wanted to set myself free.

My heart opened as I prayed for our society now – that

we learn from the thousands of stories of child abuse as they surface and dominate the media. I prayed for a safer, more nurturing society for our children, for generations to come. I prayed for an end to the extremes of sex and violence that go out in the name of entertainment. I prayed for a collective shift in our consciousness. I prayed for the world. I prayed for love.

So what of this world? And what of love?

As day turned to dusk, I gazed out at the gentle greyness beyond the balcony. There were very few glorious technicolour sunsets in Kovalam these days. Rather, the sun dropped into a horizon of smog that loomed over the sea, a menacing warning of the disregard for the planet on which we live, with its anger and its wars, with all of the greed and stupidity that threaten our very existence. It was a poignant counter-balance, a twisted metaphor for the clarity I had gained.

Life is no fairy tale.

We have illness, we have suffering, we have old age, we have death.

This is it.

Love it all.

Along with those dead cells which had clouded my thinking, my need to escape reality had also been dissolved. The veil of my romantic delusion had finally been lifted, so that I could look squarely into the face of reality, however stark it may appear. From this day forth I would strive to live in nothing but the truth. By taking this essential step of forgiveness I had found the courage to passionately embrace all of life. My happiness depended on nothing and no one. My power lay within. I had life. I had hope.

I went to see Professor Farmer the week I came home to ask if he would teach me everything he knew.

'I have to do this', I said. 'Nothing has felt clearer.'

'For as long as I'm still alive I will', he said.

So I joined with a new mentor, a teacher so accomplished

in his field that I could only aspire to be like him, on a new journey into medicine and health. Except it didn't feel so new to me; in fact it felt like the most natural transition I had ever made. *However long it takes*, I thought, *I will learn to do this. I will learn to heal others with this doctor as my guide.*

I was on my path now. An authentic path in a real world.

Just one more thing to resolve. What did I truly desire?

A fairy-tale ending or a story of enlightenment?

What was more important? What did I wish for most?

Charming Prince or Dragon King's Daughter?

Did I really dare to believe that happiness was not dependent on me 'getting the man'? That unconditional love was itself the reward? It would not only be the greatest paradigm shift in my life, having searched relentlessly for love, but also the shrugging off of a spell-binding cultural mantra that still pinned all hope for a heroine's happiness on her fairy-tale ending of sunsets and horizons.

I travelled back to Egypt to face this truth. There were tough security checks all around the airport. Islamic State fighters had just murdered twenty-three Egyptian Christians, and Egypt had launched an air attack on Libya. My taxi driver was in despair.

'It's all crazy. It's everywhere, and it's crazy.'

That's what most people feel, isn't it? No matter where they live, whatever their creed or faith, nobody wants to live in fear of being beheaded by insane terrorists or gunned down by a military force. If there could possibly be a silver lining to this arbitrary killing, to the wars, to the terrorism, to all the problems that we face in our world, let it be the realization that no one truly wants it to be this way. Let there be an end to the meaningless divisions between us. Let there be an end to the wars, the greed, the politics, the exploitation. Instead, let there be a mutual rising of our consciousness. Let there be an end to hate.

Let there be love.

It was early spring. Mina and I returned to our favourite beach, this time not riding on camels, but on a speedboat across a choppy sea with flying fish escorting us on either side. Our Bedouin friends made a lunch of rice and salad and brought it to our hut. Finally we talked it out: our feelings for each other and the obstacles that stood in our way. If he were allowed into my country he would have to turn his back on his family and it would break his mother's heart – a woman who had already lived through military dictatorship, survived violent revolution and borne three sons in a country that opposed her faith. We could never be happy if we caused such suffering.

We had to break up. There was no other option. It was done.

My tears flowed. For a short time he kissed them away. But for today we remained together. There was joy in our decision, the joy of knowing each other and of being able to do the right thing. Our love depended on nothing, demanded nothing and judged no one. It was pure. He said he was taking me to the next lifetime with him. We felt closer than ever as we held each other in an embrace that went back further than we could ever comprehend. Past, present and future all in that moment.

My morning practice the following day was only love. Love for me, love for him, love for all our neighbours, his family, my family, for my new life back at home.

I had already chanted *Nam-myoho-renge-kyo* for eight months in this Middle Eastern place, each time planting a prayer and a seed for my own life and for world peace. I had chanted the same, ten years before, on that first yoga journey. It had always been my prayer. Now it felt more crucial than ever.

As I sat in the lotus position, I focused on the clear horizon. A calm blue sea stretched out to meet the rugged mountains of Saudi Arabia in the distance. I breathed steadily. Breathe in. Breathe out. My heart lifted in joy, wishing nothing but peace and happiness for all the people living here, for the people I knew back home, for the lives of everyone. And as I took breath once more, I pictured the biggest, brightest, whitest lotus flower, floating on this stretch of water between east and west, its roots stretching deep into the ground of this beautiful abundant earth that we all share. The deeper its roots reached into the mud, the brighter and whiter and more beautiful it became. The more I felt love the more my heart lifted. And then I realized.

Nothing and no one will take this love away from me, because they can't.

I don't own this love.

It just flows through and around me.

It is not dependent love. It is pure love.

It is one love. It is unconditional. And it is free.

Epilogue

Nowhere beats London on a warm sunny day. But today the buzz was special. I stood at the SOAS college entrance and breathed in the atmosphere of the first day of autumn term. In my hand was a freshly printed ID pass. Postgraduate. Arts and Humanities. It was a new school year. My first day back into education for twenty-six years. I smiled. It felt like only yesterday.

The undergraduates held my attention in gentle amusement as I witnessed their wonderfully naïve excitement. How many of these young students were spending their first days away from home? How far had they come, not only geographically, but also emotionally, to reach this elite academic establishment? What had they experienced so far in their young but powerful lives? I wanted to sit on the steps with all of them. Ask them about their dreams. Share in their blissful optimism. Encourage the ones who were scared. Or scarred… But I couldn't do that today. Today my past was all too present.

That morning I'd received a phone call. It was the police CID again. This time to tell me that the schoolteacher had finally been charged. Fourteen allegations of indecent assault, one serious, all against children under ten years old, overwhelmingly supported by witness statements and corroborating evidence.

He was to plead 'Not Guilty'. The case would go to trial by jury within months. I could hardly take it in.

As I turned to pass through the entrance and find my first welcome meeting, I caught a young man looking admiringly in my direction. He was handsome. Young. Probably around 21. I wondered if he realized I was 47. Probably not. I still dressed the same as I always had. Skinny jeans. High-tops. Long brown hair. I took the compliment as I passed through the turnstiles into the main building. But I wasn't here for that. This time I was on a mission.

I had a purpose now. Work to do. I'd learned a lot, I'd experienced a lot, and it was time to share it. To offer healing and support. I'd need more qualifications. A doctorate, eventually. It was going to take a while, but today was the beginning.

Yet as I sat in the classroom with my new classmates, feelings overwhelmed me and I was almost mute – my head caught up in fear at the prospect of facing that schoolteacher all these years later. Another layer of trauma to heal. More pain to resolve. Would this process never end?

And so began the real business of preparing to face a childhood abuser in court. At every juncture another demon would surface. A personal demon, that is. Doubt, insecurity, shame, anger, frustration, guilt… Yes, even guilt. One by one, one at a time, I was able to transform them into something of value, something worth living for.

Finally, almost twelve months on, the trial came around.

I can't pretend it was fun, or even remotely liberating in the moment. There was a certain energy about that courtroom, along with the questions I was asked, that left me feeling vulnerable and exposed. Afterwards I became incredibly attached to the outcome. I hadn't expected the verdict to mean so much. After all, I already knew the truth. I had found my voice. Once again, I was forced to let go, to trust that I would be OK. No matter what.

Faith. What else did I have?

The verdict was unanimous. 'Guilty' on all charges. Forty years after the crime this man was sentenced to ten years in prison. I sobbed for a while when they told me, the deeply held sorrow of a little girl who was finally listened to and believed. But the tears soon evaporated, warmed by an overwhelming and powerful sense of relief. Everything really was OK. And so was I. More than OK. Through all of this I had changed something so profound, something no one would ever be able to take away. I was already living happily ever after.

What's truly important to me now is not what happens to any perpetrator, but what happens to the survivors. Not only the survivors of child abuse, but the survivors of trauma, everywhere. And it is to you, the survivor, that I dedicate this book.

Let's not just survive. Let's thrive.

Notes

Frontispiece

* 'Silent All These Years' written by Tori Amos, published by Sword and Stone from the album *Little Earthquakes*, Warner Music Group (1992). Used by kind permission of Tori Amos.

Chapter One – Hell

1 'New Years Gosho', *Writings of Nichiren Daishonin*, Vol. 1, p. 1137. Soka Gakkai, Japan, 1999.
2 Soft Cell, 'Where the Heart Is', *The Art of Falling Apart*. Sire Records, 1983.
3 Soft Cell, 'The Art of Falling Apart', *ibid*.
4 Rufus and Chaka Khan, 'Ain't Nobody', *Stompin at the Savoy*. Rhino/Warner Bros., 1983.

Chapter Two – Hunger

1 'The True Aspect of All Phenomena', *Writings of Nichiren Daishonin*, Vol. 1, p. 384. Soka Gakkai, Japan, 1999.
2 U2, 'I Still Haven't Found What I'm Looking For', *The Joshua Tree*. Island Records, 1987.
3 Massive Attack, 'Unfinished Sympathy', *Blue Lines*. Wild Bunch Records, 1991.

Chapter Three – Animality

1 'The Object of Devotion for Observing the Mind', *Writings of Nichiren Daishonin*, Vol. 1, p. 358. Soka Gakkai, Japan, 1999.

Chapter Four – Anger

1 'On Omens', *Writings of Nichiren Daishonin*, Vol. 1, p. 644. Soka Gakkai, Japan, 1999.

Chapter Five – Tranquility

1 'On Establishing the Correct Teaching for the Peace of the Land', *Writings of Nichiren Daishonin*, Vol. 1, p. 24. Soka Gakkai, Japan, 1999.
2 Richard Causton, *The Buddha in Daily Life*, pp. 137–38. Rider, 1995.
3 *Ibid.*, p. 138.
4 *Ibid.*, p. 138.
5 *Ibid.*, p. 139.
6 New Order, 'Temptation', *Factus 8*. Factory Records, 1982.
7 'The Opening of the Eyes', *Writings of Nichiren Daishonin*, Vol. 1, p. 279.

Chapter Six – Rapture

1 'Happiness in This World', *Writings of Nichiren Daishonin*, Vol. 1, p. 681. Soka Gakkai, Japan, 1999.

Chapter Six – Learning

1 'Letter to the Brothers', *Writings of Nichiren Daishonin*, Vol. 1, p. 502. Soka Gakkai, Japan, 1999.
2 Mos Def, 'Lifetime', *True Magic*. Geffen Records, 2006.
3 'Letter to the Brothers', *Writings of Nichiren Daishonin*, Vol. 1, p. 502.
4 'On Offerings for Deceased Ancestors', *Writings of Nichiren Daishonin*, Vol. 1, p. 820. Soka Gakkai, Japan, 1999.

Chapter Eight – Realization

1 'The Three Kinds of Treasure', *Writings of Nichiren Daishonin*, Vol 1, p. 851. Soka Gakkai, Japan, 1999.
2 'The Supremacy of the Law', *Writings of Nichiren Daishonin*, Vol. 1, pp. 613–14. Soka Gakkai, Japan, 1999.
3 Louise L. Hay, *You Can Heal Your Life*, p.158. Hay House, 1984.
4 'The Three Kinds of Treasure', *Writings of Nichiren Daishonin*, Vol. 1, p. 851. Soka Gakkai, Japan, 1999.

Chapter Nine – Bodhisattva

1 'The Three Kinds of Treasure', *Writings of Nichiren Daishonin*, Vol. 1, p. 852. Soka Gakkai, Japan, 1999.
2 'Never Disparaging', *The Lotus Sutra*, p. 266. Translation by Burton Watson. Columbia University Press, 2003.
3 'Sutra of True Requital', *Writings of Nichiren Daishonin*, Vol 1, p. 928. Soka Gakkai, Japan, 1999.
4 Tammy Wynette, 'D-I-V-O-R-C-E'. Epic Records, 1968.
5 'The Strategy of the Lotus Sutra', *Writings of Nichiren Daishonin*, Vol. 1, p. 1001. Soka Gakkai, Japan, 1999.

Chapter Ten – Buddhahood

1 'On Attaining Buddhahood in This Lifetime', *Writings of Nichiren Daishonin*, Vol. 1, p. 3. Soka Gakkai, Japan, 1999.
2 Coldplay, 'Sky Full of Stars', *Ghost Stories*. Parlophone, 2014.
3 Daisaku Ikeda, *The World of Nichiren Daishonin's Writings*, Vol. 1, p. 158. SGI-Malaysia 2003.
4 Richard Causton, *The Buddha in Daily Life*, p. 178. Rider, 1995.
5 'The Difficulty of Sustaining Faith', *Writings of Nichiren Daishonin*, Vol. 1, p. 471. Soka Gakkai, Japan, 1999.
6 David R. Hawkins, *Healing and Recovery*. Veritas, 2009.
7 *Ibid*, p. 46.

Acknowledgements

There have been many people who have helped in the creation of this book. I hope that I remember everyone here:

Kathryn for prompting me to write, Jess for suggesting I find an editor, Ludo and Arnaud for providing one. Catherine Adams from Inkslinger Editing in New York for your patience and brilliance. Eddy Canfor-Dumas for the strict creative steer. And Tony Morris. Thank you for making the final step so enlightening.

Thank you to the early readers of the manuscript: Pru Sowers, Matthew Phypers, Mary Parkinson. Paul Flitcroft. You encouraged me while my vision was taking shape. And David S. You held a bright mirror at a crucial moment and helped me to believe.

Gibson Blanc for the cover image. Only a true friend would get up at 2 a.m. after their wedding for 'the shot'. Tony Judge for your creative support and the spontaneous cover design. Mathew Alexander. Not only are you one of my dearest friends, you are brilliant at what you do. Debbie Costello, skin goddess. Steven Perry for a perfect headshot.

For your professional help and encouragement: Rachel Kelly,

Miles Adcox, Monnie Furlong, Adela Campbell, Greg Rees, John Greager, Gus Sellitto, Sara Giddens, Louise Leach. Florence Peake.

My deep gratitude and appreciation to everyone who has been part of my story:

Mum and Dad. Mark and Matthew. Aunty Sue. Isaac and Jacob. My small and imperfectly formed family. And to those who came before us.

Sara, Tony, Callum and Ella. Clare and Nick. Richard. Lucy. Tina. Louise and Paloma. Sean. Robert. Britt and John. Juan. Natasha. Moriam. Rose. Margie. Mathew. Mary. Florence. Nadja. Sam. Sue. David. Manju. Karine. Vinay. Camilla. John. Sophie and Jason. Joe. Wendy and Russell. Dawn. Sarah. Russell. Viv and Pip. Fiona. Myra. Jonathan. Bruce. Nigel. Rachel. Andy. Bella. Paul W. Carol. Paul C. Jacques. Imogen. Adam. Kevin P. Edward. Michael. Sean. Malcolm. Emma. Cathy. Ken. Simon. Jeff. Jenny. Steve and Matt. Stephen. Erick. Mark. Xavier. Lucie. Lola. Kev W. Casey C. Kirsten. Christine. Peter. Dan, Sonja and Imogen. Gibson and Sarah. Robbie. Georgina. Roger. Sandra. Lynette. Katie. Maithili. The Kovalam crew: Robin. Mandy. Bart. Denis. Juan. Tina. Gunnar. Ludo. Arnaud. Randa. Carmen. Rosanna. Desiree. Marcus. Mauro. Marina. Christina. Giulia. Stefano. Pradeep. Prasanth. Saji. At Onsite: Barbara. Dave. James. Leslie. Katherine. Casey. Shellie. Meadow. Scott. Travis. Ryan. Good teachers: John Pipes. Mr. Millington. Lino Miele. John Scott. Eileen Gauthier. Corrie Preece. Joey Miles. Professor Gordon Farmer M.D. Susanne Pritchard. Robert Samuels. Robert Harrap. Kazuo Fujii. Daisaku Ikeda. And Mina. Everglow.

The Maida Vale crew. There are no words. You make my heart sing.

Friends in faith: Sue. Faith. Tobi. Shoba. Max. Cinzia. Jessica. Miyoko. And ALL the spiritual rock stars of Westminster and West London. You are too many to name. There is only love.

And Lottie. You saved my life. I saved yours. You are an extraordinary intergalactic spiritual time traveller from a million lifetimes ago. And you are a poodle.

I have found the following organizations helpful in recovery. You may want to check them out.

Addiction

Alcoholics Anonymous: aa.org
UK Helpline 0800 9177 650
www.alcoholics-anonymous.co.uk

Narcotics Anonymous: na.org
UK Helpline 0300 999 1212
www.nauk.org

Sex and Love Addicts Anonymous: slaawfs.org
UK Helpline 07984 977 884
www.slaauk.org

Child abuse

NAPAC – National Association for Prevention of Abused Children: www.napac.org.uk
UK Helpline 0808 801 0331

Therapeutic treatment

Chris John: www.chrisjohn.london

Onsite Workshops: www.onsiteworkshops.com

Possibilities: www.supportpossibilities.org

Priory Hospital North London: www.priorygroup.com

Terrence Higgins Trust: www.tht.org.uk
UK Helpline 0808 802 1221

Yoga

Lino Miele: www.linomiele.com

The Life Centre: www.thelifecentre.com

Triyoga: www.triyoga.co.uk

Buddhism

Soka Gakkai International: www.sgi.org

Ruth has chosen to donate a proportion of her royalties to Possibilities Inc., whose mission is 'to aid in the healing and rebuilding of individuals, couples, and families, who struggle from the effects of trauma, abuse, stress, mental-health and relationship issues'.

www.supportpossibilities.org

For news about Ruth visit
www.ruthphypers.com

For news about Mud Pie visit
mudpiebooks.com

Printed in Great Britain
by Amazon